Coming Into Being

Sabina Spielrein, Jung, Freud, and Psychoanalysis

FRANK J. MARCHESE, PhD

Published by Frank J. Marchese, PhD
Toronto, Canada

First edition March 2015
Second edition December 2015

Front cover photograph
by Robin Mason
Prague, 2007

Author's photograph
by Robin Mason
Paris, 2012

ISBN: 978-0-9687967-5-7

To Bluejay

per sempre

Contents

Acknowledgements

WITHOUT THE HELP I received from many quarters, this book would have not been completed. I am grateful for this assistance and wish to acknowledge the following persons: Nicole Hilton for her patience and skills as an editor during the early stages of this project and R. Andrew Paskauskas, editor of *The Complete Correspondence of Sigmund Freud and Ernest Jones, 1908–1939* (1993), for providing astute and helpful comments on various drafts of the manuscript. Matthew Kudelka, who edited an early version of the manuscript. Natasha Kisenkov for making a number of useful suggestions and Anna Kiseleva, who generously provided materials pertaining to Spielrein's life and psychoanalytic work in Russia. Dr. Michel Silberfeld for his kind support and encouragement. Samita Sarkar for her thorough editing of more recent portions of the manuscript, which brought the book closer to completion. Robin Alter for providing valuable information about copy editing and publication venues. Catharine Chen for her superb work on the index. And Didi Pollock, whose excellent editorial work on the final draft and advice on design and layout were of considerable help to me in finishing what I started three years ago.

And finally, I owe a debt of gratitude to my wife, Robin Mason, who from December of 2011 listened with interest and patience to my enthusiastic and "interminable" chatter over my newly discovered interest in Sabina Spielrein. Her commentaries, encouragement, and support over these last few years were of immeasurable importance in sustaining my optimism and energy throughout.

For too long, the key role played by Sabina Spielrein in the early years of psychoanalysis has been overlooked. I hope that this book contributes to the well-deserved renewal of interest in her achievements and her legacy.

Lastly, I bear full responsibility for the content of this book.

Frank J. Marchese

December 31, 2015
Toronto, Canada

Introduction

> Where love reigns, the ego, the ominous despot, dies.
>
> Sabina Spielrein

THIS BOOK CONCERNS the Russian psychiatrist and psychoanalyst, Sabina Spielrein, her relationship to Carl Jung and Sigmund Freud, and her contribution to psychoanalysis in its early history and development. Spielrein began as a patient of Carl Jung and became a successful medical student, a psychiatrist and psychoanalyst in her own right and a colleague of Jung and Freud. Yet it has been rightfully suggested that Spielrein was never accorded the recognition she deserved for her influence on the theory and practice of psychoanalysis (Covington, 2003a). Although Freud and Jung are regarded as pioneers of modern psychology, as one historian of psychoanalysis reminded us, "in the written history of psychoanalysis we look in vain for Sabina Spielrein" (Richebächer, 2003, p. 246). As a recent biographical commentary put it, she seems to have "vanished" from the psychoanalytic literature (Launer, 2011, p. 9).

"Vanished"? Ironic, in light of what the eminent child psychologist and psychoanalyst, Bruno Bettelheim (1983), noted in regard to Spielrein. He said she was "one of the great pioneers of psychoanalysis" (p. 44). Two prominent historians of psychoanalysis, Appignanesi and Forrester (2000), concur with Bettelheim's viewpoint. They remark that Spielrein was "the first woman analyst to have a significant theoretical impact on psychoanalysis" (p. 204). And yet, for most of the twentieth century, the main record of her existence consisted of "four footnotes" in Freud's essays (Launer, 2011, p. 9).

Recently, however, there has been a rekindling of interest in Spielrein. In 2011, Canadian director David Cronenberg released a film entitled *A Dangerous Method,* about her relationship with Jung and Freud. There has also been renewed interest among academic writers such as Covington and Wharton (2003) and Allain-Dupré (2004).

In writing this book, my aim has been to bring certain aspects of Spielrein's life into sharper relief. The book offers a review and analysis of the historical portrayal of Spielrein's influence on Freud and Jung's thinking, and broadens the scope of Spielrein's place in the early years of the development of psychoanalysis. By examining her theoretical insights and her contributions to important concepts such as Freud's death instinct, transference/countertransference,[1]

---

1. Transference: "Feelings a patient has for the psychoanalyst that are displacements from [significant others in] the patient's past" (Liebert & Spiegler, 1998, p. 540). Also, countertransference: "Feelings the analyst has for the patient that are displacements from the analyst's past" (Liebert & Spiegler, 1998, p. 520).

and Jung's concept of the anima,[2] the book will help to restore Spielrein's deserved place among those early pioneers in psychoanalysis. Furthermore, this book explores the *method* that these three principal figures developed and utilized in the early days of analytic therapy as a treatment technique for mental illness. It reveals how Spielrein, Jung, and Freud were profoundly affected—individually, personally, and collectively—by the very "method for madness," or "talking cure," they employed with those afflicted with mental problems.

It is necessary to shed some light on the beginnings of psychoanalysis, especially in regard to Spielrein's overlooked contributions to the early years of its development. Just as it was with Josef Breuer (1842–1925), whose role was minimized by Freud over the years, so it was with Spielrein, whose contributions were ignored outright by the psychoanalytic establishment. Freud refashioned the history of psychoanalysis to suit his purposes, with his "Dream of Undying Fame." As Breger (2009) comments, Freud placed himself at the forefront of developments in psychoanalysis while failing to give due credit to others. It was not until 1920, in his *Beyond the Pleasure Principle,* that Freud openly acknowledged the importance of Spielrein's efforts. In 1930, in his *Civilization and its Discontents,* Freud made a further attempt at acknowledgement. There he tried to understand why he

2. The anima is "the archetype of the 'feminine' aspects of men" (Liebert & Spiegler, 1998, p. 512).

had not been receptive to her ideas years earlier (Cremerius, 2003). His admissions came eight and eighteen years, respectively, after the publication of her seminal contribution to psychoanalytic theory, "Destruction as the Cause of Coming into Being" of 1912 (Spielrein, 1912/1994).

This book is an exploration of the relationships that developed between Spielrein, Jung, and Freud. In concentrating on the intricacies of these relationships, we gain a glimpse of why Spielrein was not given due credit at the time she presented her key ideas. It has been suggested that "Freud and Jung rejected Sabina Spielrein's theory in its entirety" (Launer, 2011, p. 10). For example, she postulated an inevitable conflict between two drives: on the one hand, the drive to self-preservation, which protected the individual's personal survival; and the species-reproduction drive on the other, which pressed for continuance of the species through procreative acts. As the aim of the species-preservation drive asserted itself, it came into conflict with the self-preservation drive; for as the former pressed for expression through the act of procreation, the individual was required to sacrifice his or her identity to bring about new life.

According to Spielrein, reproduction was both destructive and creative; it was destructive of the individual's identity but creative for the continuance of the species. As Spielrein said of these two competing drives, "No change can take place without destruction of the former [identity] condition" (1912/1994, p. 174). While reproduction created a new generation, it also destroyed the original identity of both the male and female. The interweaving of the idea of sacrifice, comprising both love and death (destruction), implied that nothing new can come into being without destruction of the old order. "The individual," she said, "must strongly hunger for this new creation in order to place its own destruction in creation's service" (Spielrein, 1912/1994, p. 156). In other words, reproduction predominated over survival, since the singular aims of the individual did not always harmonize with the collective aims of reproduction. As Spielrein said, "We see that the collective desires living within us do not correspond to personal desires" (1912/1994, p. 162).

This principle, implied in Spielrein's conceptualization of the reproductive drive, forms the basis of modern evolutionary theory; as some evolutionary psychologists and biologists have suggested, we devote our energy not to keeping our own individual identity alive, but to transferring whatever we can to succeeding generations (Dawkins, 1976; Buss, 2012).

Spielrein's theoretical speculations (as presented in "Destruction as the Cause of Coming into Being") were prescient, for they anticipated developments in late twentieth-century evolutionary psychology in which sexual attraction, mate selection, and reproduction are key topics (e.g., Dawkins, 1976; Buss, 2012). As for psychoanalysis, she influenced Jung and Freud's thinking about the death instinct, sadism and masochism, Jung's concept of the anima, and the conflicting and ambivalent feelings that arise in the sexual domain: feelings of desire, anxiety, and disgust. With reference to these feelings, Spielrein said, "The joyful feeling of coming into being that is present in the reproductive drive is accompanied by a feeling of resistance, of anxiety and disgust...[These] feeling[s] directly correspond to the destructive component of the sexual instinct" (1912/1994, p. 157). Spielrein commented that the reproductive drive "consist[s] of two psychologically antagonistic components, a destructive drive as well as a drive for coming into being" (Spielrein, 1912/1994, p. 184). In the pages to follow, her dualistic conception of human nature, combining destructive and creative components, will be more fully discussed.

In summary, the purpose of this book is to present to the general reader—as well as to those specialists in the fields of psychoanalysis, psychology, and biology—a well-documented treatment of Spielrein's ideas, the interpersonal context in which her ideas and theory developed, and the importance of her relationships with Freud and Jung, which served as a source of inspiration to her interests in psychoanalysis. I gather the singular references to her from a variety of sources (e.g., Allain-Dupré, 2004), and bring these disparate citations together into a readable account of her place in the development of psychoanalysis.

In undertaking this task, I will try to answer a question raised by one historian of psychoanalysis, who observed, "We are left with the question of why an analyst who was so distinguished in the early years of psychoanalysis is not well known, why her papers are not cited. They [and she] are truly 'forgotten'" (Cremerius, 2003, p. 70). I hope that this book will bring Spielrein out from the silence that comes with being "forgotten" to a place where she is remembered. By breaking the silence that continues to surround her life and work, her contributions to psychoanalysis during its early years may be more deservedly appreciated.

I might add that the name "Spielrein," in German, might suggest "fair play." And therefore, I hope, as well, that my book honours both the meaning and spirit embodied in Sabina's name.

CHAPTER ONE

Background to A (Most) Dangerous Method

> Nothing is "given" as real except our world of desires and passions, that we can rise or sink to no other "reality" than the reality of our drives—for thinking is only the relationship of these drives to one another.
>
> Friedrich Nietzsche

SO, WHO WAS Sabina Spielrein? At first glance this question may be answered simply, though not comprehensively.

Sabina Spielrein is the subject of David Cronenberg's film, *A Dangerous Method*. The film features Keira Knightley as Sabina Spielrein (1885-1942), Michael Fassbender as Carl Jung (1875–1961), and Viggo Mortensen as Sigmund Freud (1856–1939). The film has been described by some commentators as a docudrama, as it "falls between two stools, at once an historical documentary and, at another level, a drama about ill-fated love, both of the heart and of the mind" (Aguayo, 2012, p. 1). Specifically, this film tells the story of Spielrein's relationship with Carl Jung, the Swiss psychiatrist and analyst, as well as her encounter with Sigmund Freud, the founder of psychoanalysis. This film was based in part on the available source material and may be considered, according to Aguayo, a "cinematic portal" (2012, p. 1) to the transference/countertransference to which the principal dramatis personae, Spielrein and Jung, succumbed.

Considering, however, that Spielrein was a psychiatrist and psychoanalyst, one might wonder after watching this film, what were her contributions to Freud and Jung's thinking? What part did she play in the early history of psychoanalysis? What became of her after she was no longer a patient of Carl Jung? What became of her following her professional relationship with Freud?

I will address these questions by consulting the source material that documents her life and work. Much of the archival documentation on Spielrein's life and work consists of her diary, letters, and drafts of letters that she wrote to Freud and Jung, as well as letters Freud and Jung wrote in response to Spielrein (Kerr, 1994).

A portion of these documents formed the basis of a book published in 1982 by Aldo Carotenuto, under the title *A Secret Symmetry*. At the time of the book's publication, Carotenuto was a professor of personality at the University of Rome and a Jungian analyst. Carotenuto's *A Secret Symmetry* was followed by an in-depth scholarly work, *A Most Dangerous Method* (1994), by John Kerr, a clinical psychologist and historian of the early history of psychoanalysis. The title of Kerr's book coincides with Cronenberg's film title. Here, however, we should leave nothing to coincidence.

It is important to note that the title of Kerr's book, and the title of Cronenberg's film, make use of the phrase "a most dangerous method." This phrase was most likely borrowed from the American psychologist and philosopher, William James (1842–1910), who employed it in a letter written on September 28, 1909 to his friend and fellow psychologist, Theodore Flournoy (1854–1920) (as cited in Kerr, 1994, pp. 244–245). James had recently met Freud and Jung in September of 1909, at Clark University in Worcester, Massachusetts, and he shared his impressions of that meeting with Flournoy (Kerr, 1994). Freud and Jung had been invited by the president of Clark University, G. Stanley Hall (1844–1924), to give a series of lectures as part of the twentieth anniversary celebrations of the founding of the University.

As the first president of Clark University and of the American Psychological Association, Hall was highly regarded among his peers, both academically and professionally (Marchese, 1995). Although he was a pioneering psychologist specializing in child and adolescent development, and not a clinically trained psychologist or psychoanalyst, he recognized the importance of Freud's work for general psychology. Alert and ambitious, as well as eclectic, Hall was an advocate for novel ideas in psychology; Freud's work had quickly caught his attention in the early 1900s. In his two-volume treatise *Adolescence* (1904), Hall alluded several times to Freud's ideas about sexuality (Gay, 1988). Thus, Hall had prepared the ground for Freud's visit well in advance of his formal invitation to Freud in 1909. As Gay (1988) observed, "[Hall] was an enterprising psychologist [and] far from fearing controversy, he cultivated it" (p. 206). Freud, already a controversial figure within the fields of general and clinical psychology, suited Hall's "enterprising" spirit of not "fearing controversy," and thus Hall was happy to introduce Freud's psychoanalysis to an American audience. At the Clark University celebrations, Freud was duly honoured by his hosts, receiving the degree of Doctor of Laws, *honoris causa,* which he proudly accepted September 10, 1909. Freud was delighted with the enthusiasm his audience showed him at Clark, calling the occasion "the first official recognition of our endeavors" in psychoanalysis (as cited in Gay, 1988, p. 207).

However, days prior to his arrival in America, during his trans-Atlantic voyage, Freud had quipped to his travelling companion and co-invitee, Carl Jung, "Don't they know we're bringing them the plague?" (as cited in Prochnik, 2006, p. 18), thus betraying his ambivalence about what America represented to him personally, and what he believed psychoanalysis had to offer his American cousins. Well in advance of setting foot on American shores, over the years Freud had expressed anti-American sentiments, claiming his Old World of Europe was "governed by authority," while the New World of America was governed "by the dollar" (as cited in Gay, 1988, p. 562). Gay, Freud's biographer, commented, for "Freud the United States was, in a word, 'Dollaria'" (1988, p. 568). And in 1925, when Samuel Goldwyn of Metro-Goldwyn-Mayer films was to offer Freud the sum of $100,000 US dollars to write a film on psychoanalysis, the Viennese boulevard paper, *Die Stunde*, claiming to base its story on an interview with Freud, reported that Freud responded to Goldwyn's request for an interview with a one sentence letter: "I do not intend to see Mr. Goldwyn" (as cited in Gay, 1988, p. 454).

Though Freud was well received by his American audience at Clark University, this was to be his first and only visit to America. Years later he reminisced, "We found to our great surprise that the unprejudiced men in that small but reputable university knew all about psychoanalytic literature," employing the subject in their lectures (as cited in Gay, 1988, pp. 207–208).

It is worth noting that, in addition to Spielrein, other early contributors have also failed to receive proper acknowledgement, having been similarly overshadowed by Freud. In the Clark lectures, Freud paid homage to his former colleague, Josef Breuer (1842–1925),[3] senior author of *Studies on Hysteria,* by acknowledging that he and Freud jointly published the work in 1895. As Freud outlined the essential features of psychoanalysis, he graciously offered the following admission to his Clark University audience:

> If it is a merit to have brought psycho-analysis into being, that merit is not mine. I had no share in its earliest beginnings. I was a student working for my final examinations at the time when another Vien-

---

3. They collaborated on the first treatise devoted to psychoanalytic theory and method, *Studies on Hysteria,* published in 1895.

> nese physician, Dr. Josef Breuer...in 1880...made use of this procedure on a girl who was suffering from hysteria. (as cited in Breger, 2009, pp. 1–2)

The patient suffering from hysteria was the famous "Anna O." (Bertha Pappenheim, 1859–1936). Breuer respected her confidentiality and did not reveal the details of the case to Freud until several years after Breuer had ceased to be her physician and the case had been concluded. When Breuer was treating Anna O., Freud was a medical student and only twenty-four years of age. The importance of her case was recognized by both Breuer and Freud, and they included it in their 1895 book. For the record, it was Anna O. who brought the "talking cure" to Breuer's attention, calling it "chimney sweeping," during their path-breaking therapeutic encounter of the early 1880s (Breger, 2009). Anna O. and Breuer's successful collaborative approach in the treatment of her illness, diagnosed as hysteria, predated by some fifteen years Freud's application of the talking cure with his own patients in the 1890s. Yet, in subsequent publications over the years, Freud came to limit the credit he initially gave to Breuer as a forerunner of psychoanalytic theory and therapeutic practice, and increasingly referred to himself as the sole inventor of psychoanalysis (Breger, 2009).

Overall, in light of the favorable reception he received at Clark, Freud felt vindicated of the criticism he received in Europe. Years later he remarked, "In Europe, I felt like someone excommunicated; here [at Clark University] I saw myself received by the best as equal. It was like the realization of an incredible daydream, as I stepped up to the lectern at Worcester" (as cited in Gay, 1988, p. 207).

William James's phrase "a most dangerous method" reveals the skepticism that James felt regarding Freud's analysis of his patients' clinical material in the context of psychoanalytic psychotherapy. Freud's single-minded interpretation of clinical material, such as symptoms, dreams, defenses, slips of speech, and forgetfulness, as symbolic of deeper, unconscious psychological processes made James uneasy. In his letter to Flournoy, James wrote that, although the ideas embodied in Freud's work "may throw light on human nature," he had to confess that Freud gave him the "impression of a man obsessed with fixed ideas." He continued, "I can make nothing in my own case with his dream theories, and obviously 'symbolism' is a 'most dangerous method'" (as cited in Kerr, 1994, p. 245).

James believed that the interpretation of clinical material as symbolic of deeper (unconscious) processes left too much to the interpretive imagination of the clinician. How was one to distinguish between an appropriate interpretation and a tendentious one? And if a patient might acquiesce to a given symbolic interpretation, did this constitute a scientific validation for a method based on the interpretation of psychic material, dreams, and symptoms, viewed now as symbols having unique clinical meanings (Kerr, 1994)?

Let us take an example of how Freud worked with symbols from his analysis of a dream provided by the patient "Dora" (Freud, 1905/1986). When Dora described a dream that included a jewel-case belonging to her mother, Freud insisted on its vaginal symbolism, later adding, "The box... like the reticule and the jewel-case, was once again only a substitute for the shell of Venus, for the female genitals" (p. 114). In this example, the possibility of several meanings of the jewel-case is denied and one definitive, sexual, meaning is put forward. For psychoanalysis, dream interpretation led Freud to fixed symbolic meanings of the dream content provided by his patients, as was in the case with Dora. Yet, Freud's method of "free association," whereby the patient is instructed to say whatever comes to mind (and in the case of a dream, to freely associate on a particular element of the dream, such as the jewel-case), suggests the unlimited possibilities of what a particular element in the dream may mean. It must be remembered that, according to Freud, at the base of hysterical illnesses were problems of sexuality, and both neurotic symptoms and dreams could be read and interpreted as symbolic expressions of repressed wishes and desires, particularly of a sexual nature (Thurschwell, 2009).

Freud's tendency of fixing universal (sexual) symbolism, as laid out in his *Interpretation of Dreams* (1900/1933), to psychic material, as in the above episode of Dora's dream, excludes other possibilities as to what the content of a dream or neurotic symptoms might mean. Is it reasonable to assume, for example, that a knife image in a dream always symbolizes a penis, or that a jewel-case, cave, or pocket, the vagina? Freud's approach would assume so. For psychoanalysis, then, interpretation of dreams or symptoms is a contradictory creature: Freudian symbolism suggests fixed meanings, largely sexual in nature, of the dream element (or symptom), while Freud's method of free association suggests the limitless possibilities as to what the free associations to a dream could mean as the patient retells and reconstructs the possible significance of a dream element recalled, or in the case of a particular symptom, what the latter may mean to the patient as the patient free associates on the symptom.

Freud had unshakable confidence in the analysis of dreams (and symptoms) as a way of understanding the patient's unconscious motives and desires. Freud declared that:

> The interpretation of dreams is in fact the *royal road* [emphasis in original] to a knowledge of the unconscious; it is the securest foundation of psychoanalysis and the field in which every worker must acquire his convictions and seek his training. If I am asked how one can become a psychoanalyst, I reply: "By studying one's own dreams." (Freud, 1910/1986, p. 33)

William James, on the other hand, would not likely have agreed with Freud's claim. He was not convinced of the soundness of Freud's method for the understanding of the unconscious, which relied on the analyst's interpretation of the source of a patient's hysteria. As James said, "I can make nothing in my own case with his dream theories." Further, since James felt that Freud gave him the "impression of a man obsessed with fixed ideas" (as cited in Kerr, 1994, p. 245), it is likely that James did not believe that psychoanalysis, in all respects, could qualify as legitimate science.

Freud would have rebutted such a sentiment, since he insisted that psychoanalysis was a science, an objective branch of clinical medicine.

As early as 1895, Freud sought to integrate physics, biology, and neurology with psychology, hoping to make psychology a natural science for neurologists, as neurology was his medical specialty. His effort in this vein came to be known as a *Project for a Scientific Psychology* (Fancher, 1973). In draft form, Freud began the *Project* as follows: "The intention is to furnish a psychology that shall be a natural science" (Freud, 1895/1986, p. 295). This undertaking was an attempt by Freud to place psychology within the field of psychophysics and thus, his model of the mind would be wedded to brain physiology. As Makari (2008) has noted, "He [Freud] hoped to make a psychology for neurologists" (p. 71). Therefore, Freud's aim was to employ knowledge of neurology in constructing a hypothetical model of the mind that could account for neurotic as well as normal mental functioning (Fancher, 1973). To his one-time confidant, Wilhelm Fliess (1858–1925), a physician with a tendency for bold biological theorizing, Freud wrote on April 27, 1895, "Scientifically, I am in a bad way; namely, caught up in 'The Psychology for Neurologists,' which regularly consumes me totally until, actually overworked, I must break off" (Freud, 1985, p. 127).

Freud eventually abandoned his project, recognizing that the marriage of mind and body—the union between inner psychical experiences and physiological processes—was at that time premature. In a letter to Fliess, dated November 29, 1895, Freud confessed, "I no longer understand the state of mind in which I hatched the psychology...[T]o me it appears to have been a kind of madness" (Freud, 1985, p. 152). Freud put the drafts away and never published them during his lifetime. However, throughout his long career, Freud never really lost sight of the *Project*. He strove to place psychoanalysis on a firm scientific footing, whereby neurophysiology would serve as the organic substrate of mind, encompassing normal and abnormal, conscious and unconscious, states. Neither before nor since has such an ambitious model of mind been envisioned or articulated.

It was not until 1950, eleven years after Freud's death, that Ernst Kris, "a noted art historian, psychoanalyst, and student of Freud's" (Kandel, 2012, p. 53), edited and published the *Project*. The subsequent impact Freud's *Project* has had in the field of cognitive neuroscience was nicely summarized by Kandel (2012), a Nobel laureate (2000) and neuroscientist, in the following way: "In trying to formulate a scientific psychology, Freud...[was] undertaking a challenge that was almost a century ahead of its time. Indeed, [Freud's]...goal of grounding the science of mind in biology is completely in accord with the goals we are only now pursuing at the beginning of the twenty-first century" (p. 53).

The critics still abounded years after Freud's initial attempt to create a scientific psychology, and through his continued clinical and theoretical work to fashion psychoanalysis into a science. James and other contemporary critics of Freud (e.g., Bleuler, see below), were not convinced of the scientific status of psychoanalysis. As James's remark reveals, "a man obsessed with fixed ideas" is not likely to be open to a critique of his system, and that would be contrary, at the very least, to the scientific method which emphasizes open inquiry, peer critique, and challenge.

Others were not as polite as James in expressing their reservations about Freud. Frustrated by Freud's authoritarian posture, Eugen Bleuler (1857–1939), director of the Burghölzli Clinic, said in a letter to Freud dated November 3, 1913, "No matter how great your scientific accomplishments are, psychologically you impress me as an *artist* [emphasis added]" (as cited in Kerr, 1994, p. 441). On the basis of Bleuler's comment, the question becomes, just how much can one attribute to psychoanalysis the status of science versus art? In spite of Freud's insistence, however, on psychoanalysis as science, his contemporary, Ludwig Wittgenstein (1889–1951), a noted twentieth-century Viennese philosopher and intellectual, dismissed psychoanalysis as powerful mythology, indeed considering it to be mere speculation rather than scientific theory. And yet, Wittgenstein's sister was once an analysand of Freud's and was instrumental years later in 1938, in helping Freud and his family escape the Nazis (Heaton, 2000).

As was the case with Bleuler, ambivalence surrounded those who would initially embrace and then later become disenchanted with Freudian psychoanalysis. Bleuler, despite his misgivings about psychoanalysis in his 1913 letter, had written in 1896 a very complimentary review of Breuer and Freud's *Studies on Hysteria.* Bleuler wrote that the Breuer-

Freud publication was "one of the most important...of the last few years in the field of normal and abnormal psychology" (as cited in Covington, 2003a, p. 11). However, Bleuler would have a different response to the bold assertions of Freud's that were yet to come.

Bleuler's later opinions, however, may have reflected his reservations regarding the untested parts of Freud's psychoanalytic pronouncements, which were based on Freud's persuasive powers and Freud's interpretation of the clinical material that, in the final analysis, failed to constitute scientific proof. Casting the clinical data into symbolic form and proceeding to interpret these symbols as evidence of unconscious processes left much to the imagination of the clinician, permitting the clinician's bias to operate freely as potential self-fulfilling hypotheses. Bleuler said in a 1909 letter to Freud:

> There is a difference between us...For you [psychoanalysis]...became the aim...of your whole life to establish firmly your theory and to secure its acceptance...For me, the theory is only one new truth among other truths...I am therefore less tempted to sacrifice my whole personality for the advancement of the cause...[T]he principle of "all or nothing" is necessary for religious sects and for political parties...[F]or science I consider it harmful. (as cited in Breger, 2000, p. 191)

Freud's steadfast commitment to psychoanalysis—evident in Bleuler's statement that "psychoanalysis became the aim of his [Freud's] whole life"—is also reflected in his admission to Fliess shortly after the publication of *Studies on Hysteria*. Freud told Fliess, "A man like me cannot live without a hobby horse, without a consuming passion, without—in Schiller's words—a tyrant. I have found one. In its service I know no limits. It is psychology" (Freud, 1985, p. 129).

Thus Bleuler, although supportive of Freud's psychoanalytic ideas initially, cast a critical eye toward Freud's mission to have his theory securely accepted. As far as Bleuler could tell, Freud insisted on acceptance of psychoanalysis as "all or nothing." In a similar vein, Freud's one-time collaborator and eventually-to-be-estranged friend, Josef Breuer, complained that it was not the matter of Freud's exclusive emphasis on the sexual etiology of neurosis but rather science that made them part company. As Breuer observed, "Freud is a man given to absolute and exclusive formulations" (as cited in Makari, 2008, p. 92). Breuer's perception of Freud coincides with Bleuler's: Freud was unequivocal, he expected his formulations to be accepted in their totality, even though credible, empirical support might have been lacking.

Freud also had other notable critics. In an overall review of Freud's work as of 1914, Carl Furtmüller (1867–1940), a social critic and friend of Freud's colleague, Alfred Adler (1870–1937),[4] noted, "For many years now Freud has followed the same practice in his works; he pays no attention to criticisms and arguments directed at his theories, and he

4. Adler would later split with Freud over a bitter doctrinal dispute.

continues to build on the foundations which he has laid out as if they were now confirmed by scientific evidence and did not require further discussion" (as cited in Kerr, 1994, p. 439). And Max Graf (1873–1958), a member of Freud's Vienna group, offered the following comment on the debates he witnessed during the Vienna Psychoanalytic Society meetings of the early 1900s. Graf said, "There was an atmosphere of the foundation of a religion in that room." Graf added that Freud reigned "as head of a church" (as cited in Kerr, 1994, p. 335). Had Freud, as founder and head of the psychoanalytic movement, created a secular religion, rejecting any critique of his doctrine as blasphemy? As far as Graf was concerned, he had. As for dissenters, Freud argued their failure to embrace his doctrines revealed a kind of neurotic resistance.

Believing that he saw through Freud's ploy of placing his detractors on the defensive, Jung acerbically commented to Freud, "I am objective enough to see through your little trick. You go around sniffing out all the symptomatic actions in your vicinity, thus reducing everyone to the level of sons and daughters who blushingly admit the existence of their faults. Meanwhile you remain on top as the father, sitting pretty" (as cited in Kerr, 1994, pp. 335–336). Just as Freud's relationship with Breuer came apart in the mid-1890s, so would his relationship with Fliess in the early 1900s; and his relationship with Jung would rapidly unravel by 1912. Differences in temperament and doctrinal disagreements would likely be contributing factors to the strain that arose between Freud and Breuer, and Freud and Jung, leading to the eventual dissolution of what were at one time for Freud productive collaborations and friendships.

It may be noted at this point that Spielrein and Freud's relationship was on the whole quite satisfactory from its beginning in 1909 until Spielrein left for her homeland in Russia, in 1923. She was able to avoid the ruptures that seemed to plague those intimately and instrumentally involved with Freud in the early years of the development of psychoanalysis. Freud set the stage for his June 12, 1914 pronouncement (Carotenuto, 1982, p. 123; see also p. 55 of this volume), expressing his antipathy toward Jung in a letter to Spielrein on January 20, 1913 (Carotenuto, 1982, p. 118; see also p. 95 of this volume). And when Spielrein many years later was to depart Western Europe for Russia, Freud enthusiastically testified to the respectful closeness he and Spielrein shared, in a letter dated February 9, 1923: "Your plan to go to Russia seems to me much better than my advice to try out Berlin. In Moscow you will be able to accomplish important work..." (as cited in Carotenuto, 1982, p. 127). From Freud's letter, we see that he and Spielrein had developed, over the years, a relationship based upon mutual respect. Freud had every confidence that she would carry psychoanalysis forward into Russia.

CHAPTER TWO

Enter Sabina Spielrein

> In keeping with all this is the important role played by the sex-relation in the world of mankind, where it is really the invisible source of all action and conduct, and peeps up everywhere, in spite of all the veils thrown over it.
>
> Arthur Schopenhauer

JOHN KERR'S *A Most Dangerous Method* comprises a history of the early years of psychoanalysis, inclusive of Freud and Jung's collaboration, friendship, and eventual acrimonious split. Sabina Spielrein figured prominently in this early history; she was Jung's "first psychoanalytic patient" (Minder, 2003a, p. 122), an important contributor to his thinking and to Freud's as well. As Covington (2003a) remarks in her account of Spielrein's contributions to psychoanalysis, "[I]t is likely we have Spielrein to thank...for the Jungian concept of anima" (p. 6), and, she continued, "Her most significant contribution to psychoanalysis has...been her concept of the 'destructive drive,' later to be reformulated by Freud as the 'death instinct'" (p. 6).

It was Spielrein's influential paper, "Destruction as a Cause of Coming into Being" (1912/1994), that was in part responsible for the development and reformulation of Freud's concept of the death instinct. Her "Destruction" paper, based firmly on the work of Freud, Jung, and Otto Rank, was eventually "recognized for its originality and depth of learning by the European analytic community" (Miller, 1998, pp. 45–46). Bruno Bettelheim, the eminent child psychologist and psychoanalyst, regarded Spielrein's work on the destructive impulse as a "seminal paper" in the annals of psychoanalysis (1983, p. 44). And as one historian of psychoanalysis observed, "Sabina Spielrein both anticipated and... initiated a major part of Freud's psychoanalytical discussions of man's fundamental instincts" (Ovcharenko, 1999, p. 162). Further, according to Cremerius's (2003) assessment, Spielrein's scholarly contributions to psychoanalytic theory enabled "Freud to [gain] a deeper understanding of the nature of transference, to discover countertransference...and recognize the...necessity of finding an antidote to the latter" (p. 78), as the transference process entered into the dynamic between therapist and patient.

By 1911, Spielrein had become a follower of psychoanalysis and a member of Freud's Vienna Psychoanalytic Society; she was the second female member to be inducted into this society. Her "Destruction" paper, which was her first theoretical paper, was presented to the Society on November 29 of that year. It was delivered in the presence of Freud and key members of his Vienna circle: Federn, Rank, Sachs, Stekel, and Tausk, amongst others (Kerr, 1994). At that time, Spielrein introduced the concept of the destructive drive. In a seminal work, his revised edition of *Transformation and Symbols of the Libido* (1952), Jung credited this concept as being the basis for Freud's death drive, which figured prominently in Freud's later work in psychoanalytic theory (Covington, 2003a).

In Spielrein's "Destruction" paper, she introduced Bleuler's concept of "ambivalence." This concept embodied Bleuer's belief that all mental phenomena were like chemical elements: subject to a positive and negative charge. In a letter to Freud, Bleuler wrote, "[O]ur entire life is regulated by an interplay of contrasting forces. We find this in the chemical, as well as the nervous and psychic areas" (as cited in Makari, 2008, p. 208). Spielrein agreed with Bleuler's conception, claiming that "within us, negative impulses reside close to positive impulses" (1912 /1994, p. 173). She then went on to conceptualize sexuality as comprising positive (constructive) and negative (destructive) components. She argued that "thoughts of death are contained in the sexual instinct itself" (as cited in Makari, 2008, p. 313) and thus existed beside sexuality. As Spielrein remarked, "[T]he reproductive drive… consists psychologically of two antagonistic components, a destructive drive as well as a drive for coming into being" (1912/1994, p. 184).

It was not until nine years after Spielrein presented her "Destruction" paper, that Freud acknowledged the influence this paper had on his conception of the death instinct. Even then, the acknowledgement was meagre: a mere footnote in *Beyond the Pleasure Principle,* published in 1920 (Cremerius, 2003). Although public acknowledgement of his debt to Spielrein was long delayed, Freud had written privately to Jung after Spielrein's 1911 presentation to the Society: "She is very bright...There is meaning in everything she says." At that point, however, he was not yet ready to accept her ideas. The letter continues, "[H]er destructive drive is not to my liking, because I believe it is personally conditioned. She seems abnormally ambivalent" (Freud & Jung, 1974, p. 494). Jung concurred with Freud's opinion, responding that her paper was "over-weighted with her own complexes" (as cited in Covington, 2003a, p. 3).

The "Destruction" Paper of 1912

IN THE OPENING paragraph of Spielrein's "Destruction" paper, she asked a crucial question:

> Throughout my involvement with sexual problems, one question has especially interested me: why does this most powerful drive, the reproductive instinct [sexual drive], harbor negative feelings in addition to inherently positive feelings? These negative feelings, such as anxiety and disgust, must be overcome in order to use the drive appropriately...[for] an individual's negative attitude towards sexual activity strikes especially [not exclusively] to the core of the neurotic. (Spielrein, 1912/1994, p. 155)

Before proceeding to elaborate on Spielrein's question and her intriguing response to it, we might want to consider if her question has a personal reference. Was she talking about her own sexuality, her clinical experience, the experience of members of her own family, or the general population? It has been suggested that she was likely making reference to herself (Launer, 2011), for whatever existing theories were used at the time to explain the anxiety that surrounded sex in both normal and neurotic populations (such as theories proposed by Freud, Jung, and Bleuler, among others) were unsatisfactory accounts of sexuality for her, both personally and as a theoretician and clinician. For example, one theory suggested by her colleague Otto Gross (1877–1920)[5] centered on the negative feelings that arise from the closeness of the sexual organs to those of excretion. Another theory purported that the social risks involved in sex—including attacks from rivals and fear of social exclusion—were cause for the anxiety (Launer, 2011).

Jung proposed that sexual anxiety might be linked to the fears of future conflicts of interest with children, to our sense of our offspring as rivals. In this regard, Jung said, "To be fruitful provokes one's downfall: at the rise of the next generation, the previous one has exceeded its peak. Our descendants become our most dangerous enemies for whom we

---

5. Historians regard Gross as a maverick in the early psychoanalytic camp. Jung considered him the "nearest...to a romantic idea of a genius I have ever met" (as cited in Kerr, 1994, p. 186).

are unprepared. They will survive and take power from our enfeebled hands" (as cited in Spielrein, 1912/1994, p. 155). Spielrein found one of Jung's ideas in particular appealing, quoting him in her "Destruction" paper: "Passionate longing has two aspects: it is a power that beautifies everything and...destroys everything" (as cited in Spielrein, 1912/1994, p. 155). She then went on to say that Jung's observation, implying an "unknown fear lying within erotic activity corresponds...well to my results" (Spielrein, 1912/1994, p. 156). We might speculate the results she referred to were based on her personal experiences and introspections, as well as her clinical work with patients.

In drawing upon Jung's reference to the negative side of sexual experience, it is conceivable that Spielrein was referring to her own sexual experiences in the context of the initially tender intimacy (or as she called it, "poetry,") that she shared with Jung, in full bloom by 1907 or 1908. The secretiveness and tenderness of their affair she revealed in verse: "No ashes, no coals / can have such a glow / As a secretive love / of which no one must know" (as cited in Carotenuto, 1982, p. 102).

The "poetry" they shared did not last. By the spring of 1909, their affair came to an end, with Spielrein bitterly remarking that Jung "smashed my whole life" (as cited in Carotenuto, 1982, p. 42). Yet, in spite of her professed bitterness toward Jung, Spielrein wrote to Freud on June 10, 1909, "My dearest wish is that I may part from him in love" (as cited in Carotenuto, 1982, p. 92).

There seems "little doubt that by 1908 Jung and Spielrein were engaged in physical contact," as there is much mention of "poetry" in her diary from 1907–1908 (Launer, 2011, p. 27). Thus it is conceivable that she may have been mixing theoretical speculations on sexuality with personal disclosure. It has been suggested that it was Spielrein's "erotic transference to Jung (and his to her) that led her to conceptualize a destructive aspect in the drive to love" and to sexuality in general (Covington, 2003a, pp. 6–7). Furthermore, in borrowing Bleuler's concept of "ambivalence," she may have been betraying her own uncertainties and anxiety about sexuality, for as she said, "You feel the enemy…within; its characteristic ardour compels you, with inflexible urgency, to do what you do not want to do; you feel the end…before which you vainly may attempt to flee to an uncertain future" (Spielrein, 1912/1994, p. 156).

Let's now return to Spielrein's "Destruction" paper and the question she raised in regard to the "negative and positive feelings" which, she speculated, accompany the expression of the reproductive/sexual drive. First, in addressing her question and the response to it, it may be worthwhile to present a little background on Spielrein's thinking on the instincts. In agreement with the psychoanalytical concepts then current, Spielrein endorsed two principle instincts: an instinct for self-preservation, which strives to maintain sameness and protect the individual from unwanted change, and the conflicting instinct for species-preservation (sexuality), which presses for change through mate selection and reproduction. In developing her thesis, she drew attention to two psychic structures: the ego and the unconscious. The ego, depending on the energy provided by the instinct for self-preservation, seeks to maintain its own individuality and stability and to resist anything that would impose unwanted change. The unconscious, on the other hand, depends on the energy from sexuality, provided by the instinct of species-preservation. Seeking to achieve its own aims, the unconscious is indifferent to the aims of the individual, enforcing its collective and racial aims directed at the continuation of the species. These aims are given preference over those of the individual.

According to Kerr (1994), Spielrein's thesis suggested that "Sexuality does not care what...creation 'costs' the individual...[and] from the standpoint of the ego, sexuality contains an implicit threat of [ego] dissolution" (p. 320). Therefore, Kerr claims that as the aims of sexuality (the reproductive drive) make themselves felt, they come into conflict with the singular motives of the individual, the "I." The main point in Kerr's instructive analysis of Spielrein's thesis is that "*against sexuality the ego always responds with an attitude of resistance* [emphasis in original]...and sexual desire will be accompanied by defense reactions—expressed most often by... the evocation of images of death and destruction—which represents the protest of the 'I' [ego] against its dissolution" (pp. 321–322). As Spielrein (1912/1994) commented, "The frequency with which sexual wishes are associated with images of death is noteworthy" (p. 155), as these images represent the protest of the ego to its dissolution. And in his 1999 analysis of Spielrein's thesis, Ovcharenko remarks, "The basic idea at the heart of [Spielrein's] report was a simple one... [A]ny change or growth assumes the destruction and annihilation of the former state; growth therefore has the meaning of calling attention to the destructive elements of human attraction" (p. 360). Kerr's and Ovcharenko's analyses provide evidence that there is general agreement in regards to Spielrein's "Destruction" thesis.

Covington (2003a) seconds Ovcharenko (1999) in suggesting that the emergence of Spielrein's idea of destruction was bound up with the events of the Jung-Spielrein relationship. As Ovcharenko says, "The original conception came to birth through her own suffering...from grieving over the 'mad passion' of her love for Jung" (1999, p. 359).

Covington (2003a) also suggests that, "It can be argued that it was Spielrein's erotic transference to Jung (and his to her) that led her to conceptualize a destructive aspect in the drive to love" (pp. 6–7), calling for the "relinquishment of the ego" (Covington, 2012, p. 237). In a diary entry, Spielrein recorded her conception of destruction as follows:

> This demonic force, whose very essence is destruction (evil) and at the same time is the creative force, since out of destruction (of two individuals) a new one arises. That is the fact of the sexual drive which is by nature a destructive drive, an exterminating drive for the individual, and for the last reason, in

> my opinion, must overcome such great resistance in everyone. (as cited in Carotenuto, 1982, pp. 107–108)

For Spielrein, then, the concept of love was one of a merging or loss of ego; the ego's self-interest must give way to sexuality, the reproductive drive.

Kerr (1994) comments that for Spielrein, "[S]exuality contains an implicit threat of dissolution" (p. 320). As the force of the sexual instinct asserts itself, it is conceivable that psychic processes are ruled by more than a search for pleasure (sexuality) and the avoidance of pain (Makari, 2008). That is, psychic processes may have an inherent need for stability arising from an unsettling "antagonism between the *Individual Ego and the Species Ego* [emphasis added], which is connected with the drive to self-preservation and the drive to continuation of the species" (Van Waning, 1992, p. 400). As we noted above, the ego resists change, setting up defensive reactions to ward off any potential threat to its dissolution as the destructive component of sexuality presents itself.

The idea that psychic processes gravitate toward stability was put forward in the mid-1800s by Gustave Fechner (1801–1887). Fechner was a physician and physicist who, along with E. H. Weber (1795–1878), took up the experimental study of external stimuli and their psychic representations. After years of painstaking research, Fechner published *Elements of Psychophysics* (1860/1966) which offered an innovative approach for studying the relations between mind and body. It is likely that Freud was influenced by Fechner's thinking, Freud having postulated that all drives were inherently conservative and directed at the maintenance of inner peace through the discharge of excitation that builds in the nervous system. Fechner and Freud were in agreement on the organism's need for constancy or stability. Instability was unpleasurable, and therefore a compelling need for constancy could override choices between pleasure and pain (Makari, 2008).

For Freud, the dominating principle of mental life was the "need of the organism to reach a state of tranquility by… discharging all tensions…Bliss, in the Freudian scheme, is attained when needs have been satisfied and passions spent" (Storr, 1989, p. 23). Freud postulated in his book *Instincts and Their Vicissitudes* (1915/1986) that the "nervous system is an apparatus which has the function of getting rid of the stimuli that reach it, or of reducing them to the lowest possible level" (p. 116). Freud called this instinctive drive aiming for stability, the "principle of constancy" (Thurschwell, 2009, p. 83). Maintaining inner equilibrium was, for Freud, a cardinal rule of psychic and bodily function; pleasure comes from the discharge of excess excitation arising from inner and outer sources. In this light, Freud's view coincided with Fechner's.

Decades later, Spielrein's "Destruction" thesis built on Fechner (1860) and Freud's (1895) related concepts. Thus, Spielrein's conception of psychic processes was a dynamic one. There is the self-preservation instinct that keeps the peace, offering the ego protection from disequilibrium, striving to ensure stability, as Fechner, Freud, and Spielrein suggested. There is also an opposing force, the species-preservation instinct, asserting itself in the service of procreation, and in doing so, upsetting the balance that the ego strives to maintain.

Freud and Jung were intrigued by Spielrein's "Destruction" thesis. As we noted earlier, Jung acknowledged Spielrein as the originator of the idea of the death instinct. Freud also acknowledged his indebtedness to her, citing her elucidation of the destructive drive, which in 1920 he reformulated as the "death instinct" in his *Beyond the Pleasure Principle* (Ovcharenko, 1999). Freud viewed the death instinct (Thanatos, an attraction to death, destruction, and aggression) as an innate force opposing the life instinct (Eros), emphasizing the former instinct's regressive nature in reducing excessive or unwanted excitations and tensions created by the life instinct. Jung came to view the death instinct as a regressive pull in which the ego would be dissolved for the purposes of renewal and reconstitution (Covington, 2003a). Jung's view of the creative aspect of the destructive drive appears to harmonize with Spielrein's conception of destruction; out of destruction and dissolution of a prior state, a new state, a new ego, arises. Spielrein further elaborated on the creative aspect in her "Destruction" thesis:

> Self-preservation is a "static" drive because it must protect the existing individual from foreign influences; preservation of the species is a "dynamic" drive that strives for change [the ego defends against unwanted change], the "resurrection" of the individid-

> ual in a new form. No change can take place without destruction of a former condition. (1912/1994, p. 174)

This corresponded to Freud's idea that the ego defends itself against unwanted change, against the excess excitation that might disturb inner peace.

Spielrein went on to clarify how the destructive component within the reproductive drive can assert itself:

> The instinct for preservation of the species, a reproductive drive, expresses itself...in the tendency to dissolve and assimilate [transformation of the I to the We], differentiating a new form..."Where love reigns, the ego, the ominous despot, dies." When one is in love, the blending of the ego in the beloved is the strongest affirmation of self, a new ego existence in the person of the beloved. (Spielrein, 1912/1994, p. 174)

In this passage Spielrein reveals her conception of love as a merging or loss of ego; as she says, "the blending of the ego in the beloved," and as Covington (2003a) affirms, "at the expense of the ego" (p. 9). The resistance on the part of the ego to be merged with another is an issue that Spielrein addressed. "Throughout my involvement," she said, "with sexual problems, one question has especially interested me: Why does the most powerful drive, the reproductive instinct, harbor negative feelings in addition to the inherently anticipated positive feelings?" (Spielrein, 1912/1994, p. 155). Responding to her own question, Spielrein wrote:

> The instinct for self-preservation is a simple drive that originates exclusively from a positive component; the instinct for preservation of the species, which must dissolve the old to create the new, arises from both positive and negative components. In its nature, preservation of the species is ambivalent...[T]he impulse of the positive component simultaneously summons forth the impulse of the negative component and opposes it. Self-preservation is a "static" drive because it must protect the...individual from foreign influences; preservation of the species is a "dynamic" drive that strives for change, the "resurrection" of the individual in a new form. No change can take place without destruction of the former condition. (Spielrein, 1912/1994, p. 174)

The first of Spielrein's available diaries is from around 1905–1907, and these pages contain some of the ideas that she was later to develop into her "Destruction" paper. She wrote in her diary:

> Every individual must disappear...In case of the amoeba the whole "personality" in fact literally disappears; in the case of the human being only a fraction disappears. But the instinct is always one of death, the annihilation of the personality, two individual fused into one...This is also how the resistance of every personality to the sexual instinct can be explained...[B]y destroying, a man wants to an-

> nihilate himself while the woman wants to be annihilated. (as cited in Moll, 2003, p. 21)

Thus, the sexual drive, "this most powerful drive," harbours "negative feelings" by virtue of its destructive potential for the individual: the "annihilation" that is inherent in the expression of the drive in both the man and woman. Resistance to this procreative force may result from a conflict between the individual's attempt to preserve ego-stability, or ego-identity, on the one hand, and on the other hand, the corresponding temptation to merge with another, actualizing the "anticipated positive feelings" that may come about through sexual union. Thus, striving to maintain sameness and protect the individual ("I") from unwanted change, thereby honouring the self-preservation instinct, conflicts with the species-preservation drive that presses for change through sexual union and the creation of the new.

The "Biological Facts"

A KEY SECTION of Spielrein's "Destruction" paper of 1912 was entitled "Biological Facts." Here she explained how biological facts underpin certain psychological processes. Four critical points in her argument are presented on page 39, opposite.

Spielrein drew on the reproductive behaviour of lower organisms and extrapolated from her observations of lower species, applying these "biological facts" in her attempt to understand human sexuality. She did, however, recognize

Four Critical Points in the "Biological Facts"

1. During reproduction, a union of female and male cells takes place and in this process each cell is destroyed and from the product of this destruction a new cell arises. Following the creation a new generation, many lower species e.g. the mayfly, forfeit their lives, dying off. Creation for this organism is undertaken for survival and is simultaneously destructive to the adult. (Spielrein, 1912/1994, p. 156)

2. The fusion of germ cells during copulation mimics the correspondingly intimate union of two individuals: a union in which one forces its way into another...The male component merges with the female component that becomes reorganized and assumes a new form mediated by the unfamiliar intruder. An alteration comes over the whole organism: destruction and reconstruction...occur rapidly. (pp. 156–157)

3. It would be highly unlikely if the individual did not at least surmise, through corresponding feelings, these internal deconstructive-reconstructive events. The joyful feeling of coming into being that is present within the reproductive drive is accompanied by a feeling of resistance, of anxiety or disgust. (p. 157)

4. The individual must strongly hunger for this new creation in order to place its own destruction in creation's service. (p. 156)

the limitations of extrapolating from her observations of lower species and applying these "biological facts" to human behaviour. She noted that, "In more highly organized multicellular systems, the whole individual will obviously not be destroyed during the sexual act" (p. 156). Yet, the germ cells (eggs or sperm) comprising the reproductive unit will be destroyed: "Fertilization destroys these important substances...[as the] male component merges with the female component that becomes reorganized and assumes a new form mediated by the unfamiliar intruder" (p. 156). Spielrein depicted sex as a form of invasion, leading to the destruction of genes from both partners in the reconstitution of life. Modern biology also places an emphasis on sexual reproduction as a process in which each gender tries—sometimes with astonishing destructiveness—to impose its genetic will on the other, in order to prevail in the next generation (Launer, 2011).

In the case of males, Baker and Bellis's (1995) analysis of the biology of sex suggests that not all sperm simply race to fertilize an ovum so as to be represented in the next generation. They claim that only one sperm in 100 is actually seeking the ovum after ejaculation. Of the remaining sperm, about 80% are described as "killers." These sperm chemically attack and disable other "foreign" sperm (contributed by a different male). Another 20% of sperm, they suggest, are probably somewhat old and tired already (the life cycle of a sperm cell is only a matter of days to weeks). They are more passive, and collect around the cervical opening in an apparent attempt to block the entry of sperm. "Sperm competition" along with destruction of foreign intruders is, according to Baker and Bellis's analysis, a common feature in species that rely on internal fertilization (Liebert & Spiegler, 1998).

Thus, in the context of Spielrein's "Destruction" thesis, just as a man physically invades the woman, so that his sperm invades her egg, leading to "destruction" and then a "reconstitution" of biological material to bring about new life, similarly "killer" sperm in Baker and Bellis's analysis, attack and disable "foreign" intruders in the case of multiple matings in order to ensure that a given male's sperm will prevail into the next generation. Baker and Bellis's analysis lends credence to Spielrein's "Destruction" thesis; the biology of sexual reproduction truly involves some element of "destruction as a cause of coming into being."

It is clear that Spielrein showed considerable foresight in conceptualizing the dialectic of life: destruction and reconstruction—or in Freud's terms, Eros (life) and Thanatos (death)—as inevitable partners in the drama in the biopsychological life cycle.

Thus, the feelings of resistance that arise, the accompanying "anxiety and disgust" and "negative feelings" to which Spielrein drew attention, must be overcome by an extraordinary urge, a "hunger," for this "new creation." The reference to a "hunger" (i.e., sexual drive) that Spielrein put forward anticipated by many decades the evolutionary biologist Richard Dawkins's forceful argument (1986) that "living organisms exist for the benefit of DNA" (p. 126). The "drive" to procreate, to be represented in the next generation, implicit in Dawkins's pronouncement, and anticipated by Spielrein seventy-five years earlier, demonstrates the linkage between Spielrein's biologically informed psychology and modern evolutionary psychology.

It will be remembered that Freud, in his initial work in neurology and physiology, also attempted to weave these two sciences into biologically informed psychology. In his *Project for a Scientific Psychology* of 1895, Freud stated:

> The intention [of this project] is to furnish a psychology that shall be a natural science: that is, to represent psychical processes as quantitatively determinate states of specifiable material particles... (1895/1986, p. 295)

However, Freud soon abandoned his neurophysiological program and declared that, henceforth, "I shall remain upon psychological ground" (1900–1901/1986, p. 536). Yet, similar reductionist motives remained prominent in his works, where the neuron's role as a naturalistic explanatory principle is supplanted by the conception of instinct or drive *(Trieb)* as a form of biological energy (Casey & Woody, 1983). The ambitions of the *Project* still echoed many years later, in Freud's *An Outline of Psychoanalysis,* completed in 1938 and posthumously published in 1940, wherein Freud declared that psychology is "a natural science like any other" (1986, p. 158).

In light of these statements, it is plausible to interpret Freudian psychoanalysis as a form of reductionist psychology that attempts to resolve what is human into a biological substrate of instinctual energies (Casey & Woody, 1983). And yet, years earlier, in October of 1911, Freud expelled the followers of Alfred Adler for placing too much emphasis on biology in the role of mental illness (Launer, 2011). And, the day after Spielrein presented her "Destruction" paper, on November 29, 1911, Freud wrote Jung, "What troubles me most is that Fräulein Spielrein wants to subordinate the psychological material to biological considerations; this dependency is no more acceptable than dependency on philosophy, physiology or brain anatomy. Psychoanalysis goes by itself" (as cited in Launer, 2011, p. 54).

Freud never completely freed himself from the grip of biology and its role in psychoanalytic psychology. When in 1911 Spielrein came to the podium at the Vienna Psychoanalytic Society to present the "biological facts," she stood between Freud's 1895 abandonment of his neurophysiological *Project* and his more sympathetic attitude toward biology and its place in psychology as expressed in *An Outline of Psychoanalysis* in 1940. Thus, Freud betrayed his ambivalence about a biologically informed psychology in his *Outline* and perhaps that is why in his comments to Jung following Spielrein's presentation in November 1911, Freud revealed an antipathy toward her thesis that stemmed from "biological facts" as she presented them in her understanding of the biopsychology of sex.

It was not until 1920 that Freud expressed his indebtedness to Spielrein, citing her elucidation of the destructive drive leading to his idea of a death instinct, an instinct which by definition is a biological property of the organism. In his acknowledgement of Spielrein, Freud was reconnecting with biology and with Spielrein's biologically based thesis of "destruction" as an integral feature of the species-preservation drive (sexuality), which she presented eight years earlier and to which, at that time, he revealed his antipathy.

Perhaps by 1920, and certainly by 1938, the biological paradigm was explicitly acknowledged. In a reminiscence in Freud's *Civilization and its Discontents*, written in 1930, he tried to understand his rejection of Spielrein's thesis nineteen years earlier. "I remember," he wrote, "my own defensive attitude when the idea of an instinct of destruction first emerged in the psycho-analytic literature, and how long it took me before I became receptive to it" (Freud, 1929–1930/1986, p. 120). Freud's receptivity to Spielrein's "Destruction" thesis, with its underpinnings in biology, brought Freud back to his original neurophysiological thesis of the *Project* of 1895. Perhaps Spielrein's biological thesis, as she presented it in the first quarter of the twentieth century, reminded Freud of the *Project*, a project from which he had been attempting to distance himself since the late 1890s, but to which he eventually became reconciled in the 1920s and 1930s. It will be recalled that Freud admitted to Fliess in 1895 that the *Project* was a kind of "madness." During the 1890s, and for many years thereafter, Freud cast a suspicious eye on any attempts that would rest psychoanalysis on biological foundations. He was initially not hospitable to Spielrein's thesis, which, as he understood it, would "subordinate the psychological to biological considerations." As noted earlier, Freud declared that he "shall remain on psychological ground" for "psychoanalysis goes by itself," without dependency on biology (as cited in Launer, 2011, p. 54). It is to the credit of Spielrein that Freud eventually modified his strict psychological determinism by bringing psychoanalytic psychology into alignment with biology.

CHAPTER THREE

Spielrein at the Burghölzli Clinic

> As far as we can discern, the sole purpose of human existence is to kindle a light in the darkness of mere being.
>
> Carl Jung

SPIELREIN WAS NINETEEN years old when she was admitted as a resident-patient to the famed Burghölzli Clinic, located south of Zurich, on August 17, 1904. Allowed no foreign visitors, Spielrein was placed in the Class 1 part of the hospital (Richebächer, 2003). She was a private patient; her parents paid the princely sum of 1,250 Swiss francs per trimester, wanting her to receive intensive personalized care (Lothane, 1996). Both Carl Jung, who became her primary physician at the Burghölzli Clinic, and Eugen Bleuler, the director of the clinic, diagnosed Spielrein with hysteria at the beginning of treatment (Graf-Nold, 2003).

At the time of Spielrein's admission, Jung was a twenty-nine-year-old staff psychiatrist at the Burghölzli Clinic. He became Spielrein's therapist. By the early months of 1905, Spielrein showed enough improvement to be able to begin her medical studies that spring, a mere eight months from the start of her treatment at the clinic (Minder, 2003a). Taking into account that at that time, Jung's "clinical experience of hysteria was meagre" (p. 128), her recovery was all the more remarkable, for although Jung was familiar with Freud's theoretical work, he had not tried to put into practice Freud's method of treatment, i.e., psychoanalysis. As her primary therapist, Jung initially prescribed strict bedrest, no books, no conversation, and no visitors as a protection from all distractions. These measures proved successful.

During the winter semester of 1902–1903, Jung had attended lectures given in Paris by Pierre Janet (1858–1947), as part of the continuing education program offered by the Burghölzli Clinic. Influenced by these lectures, he (and the director, Eugen Bleuler) subscribed to Janet's view that hospitalization was needed to isolate the patient from family while ratifying the patient's sense of being ill. As both Janet and Bleuler observed, symptoms tended to remit once the patient was separated from the family (Kerr, 1994). When, during the early months of her treatment, Spielrein's parents requested a family reunion, Bleuler discouraged it (Graf-Nold, 2003, pp. 164–165). He even forbade her to write to them:

> As her memories of you agitate her greatly, we are of the opinion that Miss Spielrein should not write to you directly over the next few months. In order to relieve her of this responsibility we have therefore forbidden her to write to her father. (as cited in Graf-Nold, 2003, p. 163)

Spielrein was not an average patient at the Burghölzli Clinic. During her treatment, Jung would accompany Spielrein on walks in the park of the clinic, during which he provided daily therapeutic consultations (Richebächer, 2003). It was Jung's knowledge of her background, as well as her intellectual and artistic aptitude, that may have led him to believe that she would be a very suitable first candidate for applying the Freudian method of psychoanalytic treatment. As Kerr (1994) points out, she was an "hysteric, who was at once intelligent, well educated, and in the midst of a classical delirium—all in all, the perfect sort of person on whom to try out Freud's newest ideas and methods" (p. 38). Jung later wrote to Freud on June 4, 1909, some years after her treatment and discharge from the Burghölzli, saying, "She was my psychoanalytic test-case, as it were, and for that reason I hold her in special gratitude and affection" (as cited in Minder, 2003a, p. 132). As early as the end of October 1904, Bleuler informed Spielrein's parents, "She is currently assisting one of our doctors on a scientific project, which she finds of great interest" (as cited in Richebächer, 2003, p. 233). Spielrein was also invited by Jung to participate in his ground-breaking association experiments, both as subject and research assistant (Lothane, 2003). As a result of Spielrein's assistance with the association experiments, Jung was able to incorporate the results of their collaboration into his post-doctoral thesis.

As an intelligent, articulate, and highly motivated individual, Spielrein was accorded special status. She was present at the examination of patients, was involved in diagnoses, sat with the doctors during mealtimes, and was invited by Bleuler to participate in social events held at the hospital (Richebächer, 2003). Thus, Spielrein was able to use the clinic as a place where she could have the opportunity to get a clearer sense of herself and her interests, notably in psychiatric science. She took advantage of her in-hospital residency to engage in activities related to her interests in the natural sciences and her eventual formal study of medicine at the University of Zurich.

As Spielrein's treatment progressed, Bleuler and Jung corresponded with her parents about her response to therapy. In letters sent to Spielrein's mother in January and February of 1905, both Jung and Bleuler agreed that she had recovered. Bleuler wrote, "She is largely free of hysterical symptoms and she can therefore be regarded as having recovered" (as cited in Graf-Nold, 2003, p. 168). Spielrein was officially discharged from the hospital on June 1, 1905. However, she remained an outpatient of Jung's until 1909 (Minder, 2003a).

In the spring of 1905, Spielrein enrolled as a medical student at the University of Zurich (Kerr, 1994), and she completed her medical studies in 1911 (Richebächer, 2003). She consulted with both Bleuler and Jung on her dissertation, "On the Psychological Content of a Case of Schizophrenia (Dementia Praecox)." Both endorsed her work, which was published in the *Yearbook for Psychoanalytical and Psychopathological Research* in 1911 (Kerr, 1994). Spielrein became both a psychiatrist and a practitioner of psychoanalysis, and worked as an analyst in several European cities, including Vienna, Geneva, and Moscow (Schultz, 1990).

When Spielrein became an outpatient of Jung's after her official discharge in June 1905, what had been a strictly doctor-patient relationship between her and Jung evolved into romance; the two became lovers (Cremerius, 2003). However, as the erotic component of their relationship unfolded, whatever hope each had for their relationship gave way to eventual disappointment and disillusionment, and the dissolution of their intimacy. By the winter of 1909, their relationship, both therapeutic and romantic, had come to an end.

Against the backdrop of the Jung-Spielrein affair, the available historical documentation presented by Schultz (1990), Kerr (1994), Etkind (1997), and Covington and Wharton (2003) also chronicles the story of Freud and Jung's collaboration and friendship alongside that of Jung and Spielrein's, as well as the encounter between Spielrein and Freud. These accounts reveal that just as Jung and Spielrein went their separate ways, so too did Freud and Jung, for different reasons that were largely of a theoretical and temperamental nature.

In his defense of Spielrein, Lothane (1996) disputes the suggestion of Kerr (1994) that, as Jung's lover, Spielrein was to blame for the eventual conflict between Jung and Freud, thus contributing to the dissolution of their relationship. As Lothane (1996) says, it is a "falsehood promoted...by John Kerr who claims that as Jung's lover Spielrein was at the center of the squall of distrust that led to the break with Freud"

(p. 203). According to Lothane (1996), the "Freud-Jung split had other causes...[E]volving against the backdrop of the rupture with [Alfred Adler] it had to do with disagreements over matters of doctrine, specifically, the sexual etiology of neuroses and psychoses" (p. 203). For example, Adler was not fully convinced that sexuality was at the heart of neurosis. Unlike Freud, who accorded libido or sexuality the primary role in normal as well as abnormal personality development, Adler claimed that the primary human motivation is striving for superiority in an effort to compensate for feelings of inferiority (Liebert & Spiegler, 1998).

In a similar vein, Jung and Bleuler had taken positions against what they saw as the excesses of Freud's sexual libido theory, and by 1912 "Bleuler and Jung...publicly denied sexual libido any causal role in psychosis" (Makari, 2008, p. 276). Jung, a specialist in schizophrenia, did not find Freud's libido theory particularly applicable to the disorder. Referring to Freud's paper on a German judge who suffered from a paranoid schizophrenic psychosis, Jung wrote to Freud, "The loss of reality function in schizophrenia cannot be reduced to repression of libido...Not by me at any rate" (Freud & Jung, 1974, p. 469). Thus, when theory and therapy clashed with his observations and experience, Jung was impelled to express his own ideas (Breger, 2000). All in all, it appears that there were sufficient professional and theoretical disagreements between Jung and Freud to account for the breach between them, without giving Spielrein a central role in the conflict.

Thus, the theme of hopeful beginnings, which characterized the early years of the Freud-Jung and Jung-Spielrein relationships, was followed in time by a painful parting of the ways. Various written accounts (Schultz, 1990; Kerr, 1994; Lothane, 1996; Covington & Wharton, 2003; Richebächer, 2003), as well as the story of the three principle characters depicted in the Cronenberg film, *A Dangerous Method,* testify to the history of their fruitful and fateful encounters. Also, Cronenberg's film, based as it is on available historical documentation woven into an intelligent script and stylish cinematic presentation serves, according to Aguayo (2012), as a cinematic dramatization of the interconnectedness characterizing the lives of Freud, Jung, and Spielrein during the early history and development of psychoanalysis.

The tensions and disappointments that arose between Jung and Spielrein, and Jung and Freud, laid the groundwork for important life lessons that each party derived from their respective encounters. What were some of those lessons that each came to learn?

As for Spielrein, she came to understand, in the course of her therapy with Jung, the roots of her illness, and in doing so, her life took a dramatic and positive turn. She recovered from a crippling illness and proceeded to fulfill her professional ambitions by completing her medical studies, becoming a psychiatrist and psychoanalyst, and an important contributor to psychoanalytic theory and therapeutic practice (Kerr, 1994; Covington & Wharton, 2003).

As for Jung, he came to realize the necessity of charting his own professional path and taking charge of what he believed in—vital to his ambitions and way of life. He could not, nor would not, be subordinated by authority, notably Freud's authority. Jung remarked to Freud, during the point of dissolution of their relationship, "[Y]our technique of treating your pupils like patients is a blunder. In that way you produce slavish sons or impudent puppies" (as cited in Makari, 2008, p. 279). It is clear that Jung would not be a subordinate in his collaboration or friendship with Herr Doktor Professor Freud.

And as for Freud, he recognized, as he had done with Breuer and Fliess, that idealizing someone, in this case Jung, would lead to inevitable disappointment. His *dauphin*, his son and heir, as Freud referred to Jung, was a great hope for Freud, who wished to entrust into Jung's guardianship the future of psychoanalysis. On April 7, 1907, after having personally met Jung for the first time in Vienna a month earlier, Freud said, "I could hope for no one better than yourself, as I have come to know you, to continue and complete my work" (as cited in Schultz, 1990, p. viii). As their relationship progressed, Freud judged that their friendship would be, as Jung declared, "not as one between equals but as that of father and son" (as cited in Schultz, 1990, p. viii).

It was very important for Freud, as it was of great political importance as well, that Jung was not Jewish. Recognizing that others would argue against psychoanalysis, Freud feared others would claim it was essentially a Jewish mode of explanation, that it reflected Jewish preoccupations and would be identified as a Jewish science (Makari, 2008). Freud pleaded with his colleague in Berlin, Karl Abraham, to be tolerant of Jung, for it was only through "his appearance on the scene that psychoanalysis escaped the danger of becoming a Jewish national affair" (as cited in Richebächer, 2003, p. 242). He stressed this sentiment in an impassioned plea to his fellow Viennese:

> Most of you are Jews and therefore incompetent to win friends for the new teaching [psychoanalysis]... The Swiss will save us—save me and all of you as well...An official psychiatrist and a Gentile must be the leader of the movement. (as cited in Schultz, 1990, p. 152)

As tears streamed down his cheeks, he continued, "We are all in danger...They begrudge me the coat I am wearing" (as cited in Schultz, 1990, p. 152).

Despite Freud's hope that the Swiss, and Jung specifically, would save his legacy, and despite Freud's expectation that Jung would be a steadfast collaborator and friend, a defender of psychoanalysis, his hopes would not be realized as he had envisioned (Kerr, 1994). Similarly, the hopes that Spielrein had for Jung, her therapist, mentor, and lover, with whom she imagined a lifelong intimacy, would not materialize.

Yet despite the failures, in whatever form they assumed, in both Spielrein and Jung's relationship as well as in Freud and Jung's, these three individuals were transformed in significant ways by their encounters with one another. The hopes each had for the other were sadly replaced by disappointment, conflict, and some measure of despair; and yet, their individual lives took on a new meaning, for they were freed from the illusions each harboured for the other. Spielrein managed to face her disillusionment with Jung, and this very likely—and ironically—permitted her to continue to remain generous in her feelings toward him. On the other hand, Freud and Jung were not able to have a sober reckoning with regard to whatever obstacles stood in the way of their continued relationship, and as a result they were not able to mend the breach in their relationship. Spielrein and Jung were able to have a relationship, largely in the form of correspondence, which was characterized by a mixture of friendship and professionalism. When Spielrein left Zurich and arrived in Vienna in the fall of 1911, she became closer to Freud, both intellectually and personally, and her encounter with Freud helped her achieve more fully the emotional and intellectual independence from Jung that was necessary for her personal development.

However, Spielrein never lost sight of her wish to reconcile the destructively hostile relationship that existed between Freud and Jung after 1913, as both Freud and Jung sought to make her an ally of their respective camps. Freud made the matter of allegiance quite clear to Spielrein in a letter of June 12, 1914, saying, "There will be a warm welcome for you here [at the Vienna Psychoanalytic Society], but then you will have to recognize the enemy [Jung] over there" (as cited in Carotenuto, 1982, p. 123). In a letter to Freud dated April 15, 1914, Spielrein said, "Everyone knows that I declare myself an adherent to the Freudian society and Jung cannot forgive me for this" (as cited in Carotenuto, 1982, p. 112).

Yet, allegiances did not interfere with Spielrein's ambitions. She established herself as an important contributor to psychiatry and psychoanalysis, both abroad and in her native Russia.

CHAPTER FOUR

Poetry and Artificial Illness

> We are never so defenseless against suffering as when we are in love.
>
> Sigmund Freud

AND SO, to whom might Spielrein turn for love and understanding? She had experienced abusive treatment from her parents and had no close relationship with her brothers. Therefore, Jung—as her therapist, and by virtue of the nature of his analytical approach, her confidant—assumed the role of an idealized surrogate parent and eventually became Spielrein's "poet." In a letter dated June 11, 1909, years after her therapy with Jung, Spielrein revealed the following to Freud: "Four and half years ago Dr. Jung was my doctor, then he became my friend and finally my 'poet' i.e., my beloved. Eventually he came to me and things went as they usually do with 'poetry'" (as cited in Carotenuto, 1982, p. 93–94).

From this reminiscence, we can surmise that Spielrein's transference would, in all likelihood, be an emotionally charged one, as it would arise in the course of her therapy, laying the foundation for the blossoming of the "poetry" of which she speaks in her letter to Freud. It has been suggested that Spielrein's admiration for Jung was of an "adoring kind of love-cum-hero worship for teacher and parent-surrogate," she being an "inspired, highly intelligent, and highly idealizing young person" (Lothane, 2003, p. 198). Spielrein made it quite clear in her diary that a sexual love affair, dubbed "poetry," was very much a part of their relationship. And she wrote to Freud, on June 12, 1909, "My love for him transcended our affinity, until he could stand it no longer and wanted 'poetry.' For many reasons I could not and did not want to resist... [acknowledging that a] close erotic relationship [had materialized] on the days of our usual rendezvous" (as cited in Carotenuto, 1982, pp. 96–97, 100). Spielrein also faithfully recorded the development of their affair in her diary: "He told me that he loved Jewish women, that he wanted to love a dark Jewish girl" (as cited in Carotenuto, 1982, p. 30).

Jung was equally aroused to feelings of love and devotion. In a letter dated June 30, 1908 he wrote to Spielrein:

> I must tell you briefly what a lovely impression I received of you today. Your image has changed me completely...[T]here awakens in me a feeling of beauty and freedom which has once more bathed the world and its objects in a fresh lustre. You can't believe how much it means to me to hope I can love someone whom I do not have to condemn, and who does not condemn herself...How great would my happiness be to find that person in you... (as cited in Wharton, 2003, p. 33)

Jung abandoned himself to what he referred to as an overwhelming experience of love, writing, "It is my misfortune that my life means nothing to me without the joy of love, of tempestuous, eternal love" (as cited in Schultz, 1990, p. 124).

It should be noted at this point that, as Covington (2012), an historian of psychoanalysis, has observed, the "analytic boundaries [of the doctor-patient relationship] we are familiar with today were virtually non-existent when Freud, Jung, and their colleagues were practicing. There were many instances of training analyses that became erotic relationships, as well as erotic relationships that turned into analyses" (p. 233). Covington confirms the view expressed by an earlier historian, who wrote, "[T]he blurring of the boundaries between professional and sexual or familial was the rule and not the exception" in the early days of psychoanalysis (Falzeder, 1998, p. 129). Thus, with boundary violations abounding, the countertransference from Jung to his patient at that time in the early history of psychoanalysis is more readily comprehensible. Jung loved Spielrein for her proud character, the parallel nature of their thoughts, and her ability to foretell his thoughts (Schultz, 1990). And, just as Jung became an idealized parent (parent-surrogate) for Spielrein, it has been suggested that she became the same for him in his erotic transference. As Covington (2012) remarks, "Each became an idealized parent for the other, as well as the perfect partner—their soul mate" (p. 234).

By the time Spielrein and Jung's relationship began to unravel in the spring of 1909, Jung had started to treat an attractive twenty-one-year-old woman who was diagnosed with schizophrenia. She radiated for Jung a "nymph-like sensuality often found in girls living on the edge of madness" (as cited in Schultz, 1990, p. 133). Jung recalled her "wide-open dark eyes" (as cited in Schultz, 1990, p. 134). Her name was Anna Antonia (Toni) Wolff, and, according to Kerr (1994), she was "the daughter of a wealthy family... half-Jewish, and at the time in the midst of a terrible depression...with psychotic features" (p. 271). Jung soon became enamoured with her and eventually incorporated her into his marriage and household, maintaining a romantic triangle composed of his wife Emma, Toni, and himself for more than thirty years. Jung convinced his wife that a man like himself, a man of "genius," required two types of women: one like Emma, wife, mother, homemaker; the other like Toni, destined to be the mistress and source of inspiration to a creative man (Schultz, 1990).

In marked contrast, Freud—a man of very different temperament—maintained that the genius or intellectual elite must live in accordance with the principle, the necessity, of sacrificing the baser instincts for finer, higher purposes. In Freud's view, the goal of human existence, the only path to a life of refinement and culture, was the suppression of sexual impulses. Receiving limited satisfaction from sex was the fate of the civilized human being (Schultz, 1990).

It is apparent that a considerable difference existed between Jung and Freud on the matter of sexuality in the life of the individual, notably on those destined to advance civilization. While listening to Bizet's *Carmen*, Freud remarked to his wife Martha, "The mob give vent to their appetites, and we deprive ourselves...and this habit of constant suppression of natural instincts gives us the quality of refinement" (as cited in Schultz, 1990, p. 143). Yet, it is refinement at a cost, as Freud made evident: "[After] three, four, or five years, marriage ceases to furnish the satisfaction of the sexual needs... since all the contraceptives...impair sexual enjoyment... disturb the finer sensibilities of both partners...even act as a direct cause of illness" (as cited in Schultz, 1990, p. 142). Anxiety neurosis, Freud maintained, was the result of unsatisfying sexual practices, the purpose of which was to stem the tide of unwanted pregnancies. Although in agreement with Freud on the problematic nature of certain sexual practices to prevent, as Jung said, "the blessing of too many children" (as cited in Schultz, 1990, p. 142), Jung also believed that the "requisite for a good marriage...is the license to be unfaithful" (as cited in Schultz, 1990, p. 140). For Jung, the potential for "poetry" was ubiquitous. With Toni Wolff as with Sabina Spielrein, Jung made no attempt to conceal his liaison from his wife. In Toni's case, he even forced Emma and his family to accept her presence in the home. Both Emma and Toni eventually became analysts and followers of Jungian psychology (Schultz, 1990).

As for Spielrein, desperate to overcome her unhappiness at the dissolution of her intimate relationship with Jung, she wrote to Freud on May 30, 1909, "I would be most grateful to you if you would grant me a brief audience!" (as cited in Carotenuto, 1982, p. 91). However, Freud declined Spielrein's request (Covington, 2003a). Three years later, in the spring of 1912, Spielrein tried to go into analysis with Freud in order to resolve her feelings for Jung, the man, she recorded in her diary on February 5, 1912, who had "smashed my whole life" (as cited in Carotenuto, 1982, p. 42). Though warmly received by Freud as a colleague and correspondent, Spielrein never became Freud's patient or analysand (Minder, 2003a).

Following her letter dated May 30, 1909, Spielrein wrote to Freud on June 11, 1909, revealing that Jung had proceeded from being her doctor to her lover. She also included in this letter that Jung "preached polygamy; his wife...[has] no objection" (as cited in Carotenuto, 1982, p. 93).

Some years earlier, Jung had composed a report to Freud about "Fräulein Spielrein," and concluded his report as follows:

> In the course of her treatment the patient had the bad luck to fall in love with me. She continues to rave blatantly to her mother about this love and her secret spiteful glee in scaring her mother is not the least of her motives. Therefore, the mother would like, if needed, to have her referred to another doctor, with which I naturally concur. (as cited in Lothane, 1996, p. 205)

The report was not delivered to Freud, but rather was given to Spielrein's mother in the event that she wished to proceed with a referral for continued treatment of her daughter by someone other than Jung. It may be noted that this report, dated September 25, 1905, was written two years before Freud and Jung met personally in March of 1907 in Vienna.

Correspondence between Freud and Jung started in 1906, and in his second letter to Freud, dated October 23, 1906, Jung anonymously mentioned Spielrein for the first time:

> At risk of boring you, I must abreact[6] my most recent experience. I am currently treating an hysteric with your method. Difficult case, a 20-year-old Russian girl student, ill for 6 years. First trauma between third and fourth year. Saw her father spanking her older brother on the bare bottom. Powerful impression. Couldn't help thinking afterwards that she had defecated on her father's hand. From the fourth–seventh year convulsive attempts to defecate on her own feet, in the following manner: She sat on the floor with one foot beneath her, pressed her heel against her anus, and tried to defecate and at the same time to prevent defecation. Often retained the stool for 2 weeks in this way! Has no idea how she hit upon this peculiar business; says it was completely instinctive, and accompanied by blissfully shuddering feelings. Later this phenomenon was superseded by vigorous masturbation. I should be extremely grateful if you

---

6. Abreaction is the "process of expressing long pent-up emotion about a previously forgotten event...[It] was recognized by Freud to be an important therapeutic agent. If abreaction occurred, relief of symptoms almost always followed" (Fancher, 1973, p. 52).

> would tell me in a few words what you think of this story. (Freud & Jung, 1974, p. 7)

Freud immediately responded to Jung's letter saying:

> I am glad to hear that your Russian is a student; uneducated persons are at present too inaccessible for our purposes. The defecation story is nice and suggests numerous analogies...It must be possible, by the symptoms and even by the character, to recognize anal excitation as a motivation. Such people often show typical combinations of character traits. They are extremely neat, stingy, and obstinate, traits which are in a manner of speaking the sublimation of anal eroticism. Cases like this based on repressed perversion can be analyzed very satisfactorily. You have not bored me in the least. I am delighted with your letters. (Freud & Jung, 1974, pp. 7–8))

Three years later, on March 7, 1909, Jung wrote to Freud, describing Spielrein as the

> woman patient, whom years ago I pulled out of a very sticky neurosis, [who] had violated my confidence and my friendship in the most mortifying way imaginable. She had kicked up a vile scandal solely because I denied myself the pleasure of giving her a child. I always acted the gentleman towards her...I nevertheless don't feel clean, and that is what hurts me most because my intentions were always honorable...Meanwhile I have learnt an unspeakable amount of marital wisdom, for until now I had

> a totally inadequate idea of my polygamous components despite a self-analysis. (Freud & Jung, 1974, p. 207)

If Freud, up until that point, had noted the transference operating in the direction of patient to analyst, after Jung's letter he would take note of a transference that was operating from the analyst to the patient. Freud aptly remarked that the analyst can be "scorched by the love with which we operate—such are the perils of our trade" (Freud & Jung, 1974, p. 210).

The lessons that Jung professed to have learned, comprising "an unspeakable amount of wisdom," are commensurate with Josef Breuer's reflections on the cathartic treatment he introduced to patient Anna O. (see p. 13) in the early 1880s, evident in Breuer's letter to Auguste Forel in November 1907. Breuer wrote:

> At the time I learned a...great deal: much that was of scientific value, but something of practical importance...namely, that it was impossible as a "general practitioner" to treat a case of that kind without bringing his activities and mode of life completely to an end. I vowed at the time that I would *not* go through such an ordeal again. (as cited in Kerr, 1994, p. 193)

Breuer's wife, Mathilde, although not mentioned in the letter to Forel, not only sensed Anna O.'s affection for Breuer, but also recognized that her husband was succumbing as well to a transference-love for Anna O. Mathilde Breuer made her husband choose between her and Anna O.; Breuer chose to remain in his marriage (Cremerius, 2003). Subsequently, Breuer withdrew his treatment from Anna O. and made referrals on her behalf.

Anna O., on learning that Breuer would bring his treatment to an end, underwent a severe reaction to Breuer's announcement. After Breuer bade her goodbye, he was fetched back later that evening. Anna O. was in a highly agitated state and, according to Ernest Jones (1961), was in the "throes of a hysterical childbirth (pseudocyesis)...the termination of a phantom pregnancy that had been invisibly developing in response to Breuer's ministrations" (p. 203). Though profoundly shocked, Breuer managed to calm her down by hypnotizing her, and then proceeded to flee the house. Shortly thereafter, Anna O. plunged into a severe crisis, developed a dependency on morphine, and was admitted to an asylum on July 21, 1882 (Makari, 2008). However, Breuer did not desert his patient; he remained involved with her treatment for several years (Breger, 2009).

Eventually, Anna O. recovered and went on to become a leader in the feminist movement in Germany (Kandel, 2012). She devoted herself to the abolition of white slavery, sponsored the training and education of less fortunate young women, and eventually became known as the first social worker in Germany. In 1945, a postage stamp was issued by the government in her honour, one of a series titled "Helpers of Humanity" (Breger, 2009).

Similarly, following her therapy and affair with Jung, Spielrein used her recovery creatively and went on to be an important and innovative voice through her publications in psychoanalytic theory and practice, and as well, an important force in the development of psychoanalysis in her native Russia during the 1920s and 1930s.

Freud was especially pleased that Spielrein chose to return to Russia, in 1923. He expressed the opinion that in Moscow she would be able to do important work in advancing his own cause (Carotenuto, 1982, p. 127). By this time, Spielrein was already a wife and mother, having married Russian physician Pavel Scheftel in June of 1912. Her influence in psychoanalytic circles would certainly have been greater had it not been for the "mincing machine of Stalinist repression" (Ovcharenko, 1999, p. 367), which eventually led to the abolition of the Russian Psychoanalytic Society in July of 1930. Psychoanalytic work was labelled a crime against the state. And yet, at some considerable personal risk, Spielrein continued her psychoanalytic practice. In 1942, however, her extraordinary life came to a tragic end. In her hometown of Rostov-on-Don, Spielrein and her two daughters, along with other Jews, were rounded up by the Nazis, taken to a synagogue, and shot (Covington, 2003a).

We might speculate that Anna O. and Spielrein, no longer caught in the grip of disabling neurosis, were able to invest their respective energies through sublimation; the creative forces within their personalities were put to altruistic, productive, and socially useful ends. Each made an active and distinctive contribution to the development of psychoanalytic theory and practice.

As we have seen (p. 13), Anna O. is credited with the phrases "talking cure" or "chimney sweeping," which Breuer referred to at the time of her treatment in the 1880s as "catharsis" (Gay, 1988, pp. 65–66). Eventually, the talking cure became the method Freud developed in the 1890s, which Freud then called "free association." Having tried hypnosis initially, Breuer encouraged Anna O. to simply talk in order to give full expression to all thoughts and feelings associated with her symptoms. Talking, accompanied by a full "abreaction," that is, the cathartic method, allowed Anna O., as well as other patients on whom Breuer and Freud reported in *Studies on Hysteria* (1895/1957), to "cry oneself out" (*sich ausweinen*; Lothane, 1996, p. 207).

The transference that both Anna O. and Breuer experienced in the context of Anna O.'s therapy of the 1880s, the "artificial illness" to which they both succumbed, nevertheless bore fruit. Inducing a transference neurosis, as Breuer had inadvertently done, healed Anna O.'s authentic neurosis in the course of treating the artificial one, the latter being an artifact of the therapy itself. However, Breuer himself was no more immune to the very process that he unleashed in Anna O.'s therapy; his own hysteria became part of the dynamic in his countertransference with Anna O. The phrase "physician heal thyself" resonates in the Breuer-Anna O. episode, for what Breuer had done for her influenced and benefitted Breuer himself, through the understanding he gained of himself and of his method of treatment. Recognizing its significance years later during the preparation of *Studies on Hysteria,* Breuer said to Freud apropos of the transference phenomenon, "I believe that this is the most important thing we both have to make known to the world" (as cited in Szasz, 1963, p. 440). Freud also contended that the chief instrument of therapy available to psychoanalysts was this "analytic transference" or "artificial illness."

During the early years of the development of psychoanalysis, Karl Kraus (1874–1936), a witty Viennese polemicist and a contemporary of Freud, made an observation that is certainly applicable to the "dangerous method" discussed in this book. Kraus said, "Psychoanalysis is itself that mental illness of which itself is the cure" (as cited in Szasz, 1990, p. 89). An amusing quip, certainly, and yet it rings true, insofar as the analytical transference, termed by Freud an "artificial illness," is an integral feature of psychoanalytic psychotherapy for both analyst and patient. Breuer, for example, arrived at important insights into the dynamics of psychotherapy through the "madness in the method" that he employed in treating Anna O., a method which Freud later called "psychoanalysis."

Spielrein continued to be a subject of Jung's correspondence with Freud. Freud wrote to Jung on July 7, 1909 concerning the issue of the doctor-patient relationship and the presence of transference and the consequences of the latter:

> Such experiences, though painful, are necessary and hard to avoid. Without them we cannot really know life and what we are dealing with. I myself have never been taken in so badly, but I have come very close

> to it a number of times and had a narrow escape... They help us to develop the thick skin we need to dominate "countertransference," which is after all a permanent problem for us; they teach us to displace our own affects to best advantage. They are a "blessing in disguise." (Freud & Jung, 1974, pp. 230–231)

It is likely that Freud was recalling here the lessons he had learned while treating Dora:

> I did not succeed in mastering the transference in good time...I was deaf to the first note of warning, thinking I had ample time before me...[T]he transference took me unawares...I promised to forgive her for having deprived me of the satisfaction of affording her a far more radical cure for her troubles. (Freud, 1905/1986, pp. 118–120)

Freud treated Dora in the fall of 1900 and broke off treatment in December of that year (Gay, 1988). He was reluctant to publish her case and only did so some years later (1905/1986) under the title *Fragment of an Analysis of a Case of Hysteria*. Freud's treatment of Dora was by other accounts, "unsympathetic and aggressive" (Breger, 2000, pp. 158–159). Freud had little sympathy for or understanding of her reactions when unwanted sexual advances were forced on her by an older married man, whose wife, once Dora's friend and confidante, was her father's mistress. Although his treatment of Dora failed, it was through this case that Freud formulated his theory of transference, as a way of understanding Dora's choice to abandon treatment after only three months and her anger with him for not having cured her (Breger, 2000).

Jung's reaction to Spielrein, as Freud had come to understand it, was similar to Freud's own experience with Dora, and suggested to Freud what he had earlier called "mirror transference," now renamed "countertransference" (Lothane, 2003, p. 209). Significantly, this was the first time the expression "countertransference" appeared in psychoanalytic literature (Cremerius, 2003). Later, in March 1910, in a lecture titled "The Future Prospects of Psycho-Analytic Therapy" given at the second International Psychoanalytic Congress, Freud announced that because of "other innovations in technique related to the physician himself," we have "become aware of the 'counter-transference,' and it is this that the physician should recognize in himself and overcome" (Freud, 1910/1986, p. 144). This was something Freud had not been able to do in his sessions and relationship with Dora. Freud went on to recommend that the physician should engage in a self-analysis while making observations on his own patients: "Anyone who fails to produce results in self-analysis of this kind may at once give up any idea of being able to treat patients by analysis" (Freud, 1910/1986, p. 144).

What Freud may have been suggesting here is that, by virtue of the analytic process itself, the analyst must, through self-analysis, note the operation of what is seen as the analyst's own artificial neurosis, the analyst's countertransference, which, in the case of Jung's relationship with Spielrein, blossomed into "poetry." As the analyst comes to grips with countertransference as it emerges in his treatment of the patient, and by virtue of the potential for the analyst's own transference, the analyst is in a better position to understand himself or herself and the patient's impact on the analyst's neurosis.

It is imperative for the analyst to recognize that the patient is induced to fall in love by the analytic situation and not by the charms of the analyst's own person. As Spielrein projected her affections onto Jung, affections based on her earliest attachments, so his countertransference was similarly based on his earliest experiences with significant others, some of whom fulfilled his psychic needs and others who were disappointing; in that respect, Spielrein may be seen as repairing those disappointments with her love and devotion for Jung. As Freud noted in 1920, the analytic situation and the resulting transference reproduces "with un-wished-for exactitude...some portion of infantile sexual life—of the Oedipus complex...and its derivatives" (as cited in Cremerius, 2003, p. 74) re-enacted in the drama unfolding between the analyst and the patient. The analyst and patient may be seen as partners in producing an "emotional correction" that is embedded in the transferences taking place, a correction that must be seen for what it is by both the analyst and patient as a feature of the analytic process itself. If both the analyst and patient are engaged in a therapeutic alliance, this may facilitate the emotional correction; in the context of the transferences that are transpiring, each participant provides, inescapably, in some measure, for the other's emotional needs.

One way of conceptualizing the hysteria of a patient like Spielrein is to understand the disorder as Nasio (1988) suggested. For Nasio, hysteria is an "unhealthy bond linking the hysteric to another person—in particular, with regard to treatment, to that other who is the psychoanalyst" (Nasio, 1988, p. 1). What is left out of Nasio's formulation, however, is the role of the psychoanalyst, whose own hysteria, through countertransference, may be a contributor to this "unhealthy bond." And, as in the case of Jung, his contribution to what had transpired between him and Spielrein can be understood as his countertransference neurosis. That Jung may equally qualify as hysteric may be inferred in his confession to Spielrein. At the beginning of December 1908 he wrote to her of his love and begged, "Return to me in this moment of my need, some of the love and guilt and altruism I was able to give to you at the time of your illness. Now it is I who am ill" (as cited in Schultz, 1990, p. 124). On the basis of Jung's admission to Spielrein of his "illness," we might argue that a role reversal took place in Spielrein's therapy. Spielrein the patient is requested to be the therapist for Jung; he was importuning Spielrein to give back the love and altruism he was once able to give to her.

The erotic transference between Spielrein and Jung was fully evident at this point. Given that both Spielrein and Jung were hysteric in the context of their therapeutic relationship, one might conclude along with Nasio (1988) that, in the analytic process, "Psychoanalysis and hysteria are so inextricably linked" that

> the governing principle of analytic therapy is this: to treat hysteria, we have to create another hysteria artificially. The psychoanalysis of any neurosis, when all is said and done, is just an artificial setting up of a hysterical neurosis and its final resolution. If, by the end of analysis, we overcome this new, artificial neurosis—one that was entirely created between patient and analyst—then at the same time we shall have resolved the neurosis that initially brought the patient into treatment. (p. xxii)

Thus, through the dynamic of transference and countertransference, Spielrein and Jung found each other in an erotic, hysterical transference—though not exclusively erotic—that led at one point in the analytic process to succumbing to a madness; an "unhealthy bond" in Nasio's terms, an artificial illness, set in motion by the analytic process itself and inherent in the very method that would promise relief of her (and their respective) ills. If there is "method in madness," I suggest that there is *madness in the method* that was used to treat Spielrein's hysterical neurosis.

In the new year of 1909, rumours circulated in Zurich and Vienna that Jung was having an affair with a patient—a rumour that Jung suspected was being put about by Spielrein herself. As a result of this rumour, Jung was urged by the Burghölzli Clinic directorate to leave its service. In a letter dated March 7, 1909, Jung requested that the senior executive officer release him from his post (Richebächer, 2003). By the spring of 1909, anonymous letters were sent to Spielrein's mother saying that she should rescue her daughter, who would otherwise be ruined by Jung (Lothane, 1996). It was also during this time, when Jung was professing his desperate love for Spielrein and admitting his own illness, that his wife, Emma, was expecting their third child. Or as Spielrein herself put it, "At the time our poetry began, Jung had two girls and the potentiality for a boy" (as cited in Carotenuto, 1982, p. 100). The anonymous letters may very well have been written by Emma who discerned that an affair was taking place between her husband and Spielrein.

On May 30, 1909, Spielrein, as we have seen (p. 61), wrote her letter to Freud requesting an "audience" (as cited in Carotenuto, 1982, p. 91). And although Freud initially declined her request, he immediately dispatched a telegram to Jung asking if Spielrein was in fact the subject of his earlier letter, which had been framed merely as a disinterested request for Freud's guidance in an unnamed clinical case. Jung's response (discussed above, p. 64) was to claim that Spielrein had attempted to seduce him and, in revenge for his rejecting her, was now spreading rumours about him. By mid-June, however, Jung changed his approach. He happily wrote to Freud on June 21, 1909, that he had had "too black" a view of things, that Spielrein had come to see him and they had had a "decent talk" (Freud & Jung, 1974, pp. 236–237), and that it transpired that she was not the source of the rumours

(Lothane, 2003). Freud then wrote to Spielrein on June 24, 1909, saying:

> I have today learned something of Dr. Jung himself about the subject of your proposed visit to me, and now I see I may have divined some matters correctly but that I had construed others wrongly and to your disadvantage. I must ask your forgiveness on this latter count...Please accept this expression of my entire sympathy for the dignified way in which you have resolved the conflict. (as cited in Carotenuto, 1982, p. 115)

At this point, some degree of stasis existed in the relationships between Spielrein, Jung, and Freud. Freud could still hope, for the time being, that Jung, his "crown prince," as Gay put it (1988, p. 198), might still be depended on to protect his life's work.

CHAPTER FIVE

"The Rest Is Silence"

> To put meaning in one's life may end in madness but life without meaning is the torture of restlessness and vague desire—it is a boat longing for the sea and yet afraid.
>
> Edgar Lee Masters

AS THE SPIELREIN-JUNG affair drew to a close in the early months of 1909, one might ask, what did each gain from the dynamic that was set in motion within their therapeutic relationship? Before we address this question directly, let us turn first to Jung's conception of hysteria and how this figured in his diagnosis and treatment of the condition in Spielrein.

When Jung started treating Spielrein in the fall of 1904, he was familiar with Freud's method as set out in Breuer and Freud's *Studies on Hysteria* (1895/1957), as well as in Freud's *The Interpretation of Dreams* (1900/1933). In keeping with Freud's approach, which emphasized the recovery of painful memories and their abreaction, Jung reported that it is to the

> credit of Freud...and also Breuer...that they have amply demonstrated this fact [i.e., that forgetting is

> equated with repression] in hysterical patients. The validity of this can be doubted only by someone who has not himself tested Freudian psychoanalysis. [The] investigations [i.e., Franz Riklin's and Jung's association experiments] fully confirm the correctness of Freud's teachings..." (Jung 1905/1973, para. 657)

However, while Freud claimed that "hysterics suffer mainly from reminiscences" (Breuer & Freud, 1895/1957, p. 7), Jung did not specifically trace the root of the hysterical complex back to memory. Jung believed that when memory was traumatic, it became dissociated from affect. This dissociation led to somatization of the affect; that is to say, it resulted in physical symptoms. The notion of dissociation in hysteria and the influence of affects were shared by others, notably Pierre Janet. Jung (1903) commented that:

> Janet found that the influence of affects is seen most clearly in hysterical persons, and that it produces a state of dissociation in which the will, attention, ability to concentrate are paralyzed and the higher psychic phenomena are impaired in the interest of the lower; that is, there is displacement towards the automatic side, where everything that was formerly under the control of the will is now set free. (as cited in Minder, 2003b, pp. 113–114)

Agreeing with Janet, Jung (1906) stated that "the complex has an abnormal autonomy in hysteria and a tendency to an active separate existence" (as cited in Minder, 2003b, p. 113).

If we consider the case of Spielrein, it is clear that she displayed a host of symptoms that would testify to a lack of control of the will, which wreaked havoc in her daily life. Further, Jung (1906) emphasized, "Owing to the strength of their affects, hysterical persons are always their own victims" (as cited in Minder, 2003b, p. 112). Jung reported that his patient Spielrein "laughs and cries in a strangely mixed compulsive manner...alternating constantly between laughter, weeping, jerking of the head; seductive glances...after these excesses sometimes a severe depressive reaction" (as cited in Minder, 2003a, p. 121).

Utilizing the Breuer-Freud approach, Jung encouraged Spielrein to talk freely and in doing so, according to Graf-Nold, Spielrein found relief, having "confessed her shameful secrets, her hidden thoughts and feelings" (2003, p. 171), which had tormented her for so long. Employing Breuer and Freud's cathartic method, Jung was able to report as early as January 1905, a mere six months into treatment, the following: "Since the last abreaction substantial improvement. Still strongly emotional and unusually powerful expressions of feeling. At every stimulation of the complex she still reacts with her back, hands, tongue and mouth, though significantly less so" (as cited in Minder, 2003a, p. 124). The core complex that Jung was able to identify was based on his recognition of the roots of her symptoms:

> Basically all her gestures of revulsion and her negative behavior can be traced back to this complex [sexual association with the physical trauma she suf-

> fered at the hands of her father]. She sees herself as a thoroughly bad and corrupt person. (as cited in Minder, 2003a, pp. 123–124)

It was only after the sexual components of Spielrein's confessions were identified, that Jung was able to report significant improvement in her condition, in January of 1905 (Minder, 2003a). Given Jung's devotion, patience, and enthusiasm for his patient, Spielrein's recovery followed a steady upward course over the duration of her treatment.

It is to Bleuler's credit, that when he took over the direction of the Burghölzli Clinic in 1901, he emphasized to staff that there were three tools for treating the psyche: patience, calmness, and inner goodwill towards the patients (Covington, 2003b). Jung adopted these tools and provided Spielrein with the essential therapeutic support that enabled her to entrust her wellbeing into his care. Furthermore, Bleuler managed the Burghölzli Clinic as a residential "therapeutic community" (Graf-Nold, 2003, pp. 148–149). He passionately believed that activities that the patient experienced as meaningful had a powerful therapeutic effect. Patients, families, and staff members were all considered active members of the clinic community.

In turn, as a member of that community, Spielrein received from the Burghölzli Clinic what she was unable to receive from her parents: devotion and care for her wellbeing. By February 1905, Bleuler, echoing Jung's earlier report from January 1905, informed Spielrein's mother that "she [Spielrein] is largely free of hysterical symptoms and she can therefore be regarded as having recovered" (as cited in Graf-Nold, 2003, p. 168). Three months later, on April 29, 1905, Jung commented, "In the last few weeks distinctly improved and increasingly calm. Now listens to lectures conscientiously and with interest (zoology, botany, chemistry, physics). Fluctuations in mood still occur from time to time, particularly in connection with letters from home" (as cited in Graf-Nold, 2003, p. 168). Spielrein's recovery took place rapidly and with astonishing success. Following a mere ten months of treatment, she was able to leave the clinic in June 1905, get an apartment in the city of Zurich, and commence her studies in medicine at the University of Zurich.

Throughout the eventful years of 1904–1905, Jung was dedicated to Spielrein's recovery. He encouraged her to talk freely and thus to become an active participant in the therapeutic process. By late 1904 or early 1905, he recognized that she was showing significant improvement. Through his subsequent treatment of her, and in their friendship and collaboration, she continued on her trajectory toward recovery. Jung wrote to her in 1908, "Never lose the hope that work done with love will lead to a good end" (as cited in Lothane, 2003, p. 217).

Jung's sentiment resonated with Freud, who had written to Jung in December 1908 regarding the matter of the dynamics of transference during the course of therapy. Freud wrote, "Essentially, one might say, the cure is effected by love" (Freud & Jung, 1974, pp. 12–13); that is, a healing occurs through love. Freud was commenting here on the doctor-patient relationship, which he saw as reciprocal in nature and with which Jung was acquainted with through Freud's writings, notably *Studies on Hysteria*:

> We make [the patient] himself into a collaborator, induce him to regard himself with the objective interest of an investigator, and thus push back the resistance...One works to the best of one's power...as a teacher...as a father confessor who gives absolution...by a continuance of his sympathy and respect after the confession has been made. One tries to give the patient human assistance...and by the amount of sympathy that one can feel for the particular case...
>
> Besides the intellectual motives which we mobilize to overcome the resistance, there is an affective factor, the personal influence of the physician, which we can seldom do without. (Breuer & Freud, 1895/1957, pp. 282–283)

Jung's treatment of Spielrein's hysteria was guided by his understanding that it is through the strengthening of the ego, by introducing some new complex, that one can liberate the ego from being dominated by the complex of illness. Jung maintained that the complex of illness had an abnormal autonomy in hysteria (Covington, 2003b). As Jung remarked, "A purposive treatment of hysteria must...strengthen what has remained of the normal ego..." (as cited in Covington, 2003b, p. 183), for in hysteria, it is as if a new morbid personality is gradually created that devours what is left of the normal ego, forcing it into a secondary—oppressed—complex. When the ego is strengthened, old defenses are let go. It is the introduction of a new complex that Jung cited as the curative factor—this over and above the uncovering of and working through trauma which, Freud argued, enabled patients to differentiate from their past. By utilizing the word-association procedure, Jung was able to uncover Spielrein's problematic complex and help her to recover her memory of abuse and to experience the emotional—cathartic—release that followed the recovery of her painful memories. Through this recovery process, Spielrein's need to somatize her distressing feelings coupled with her acting out of her abusive past was markedly reduced.

During this time, Jung took note of Spielrein's father complex, coming to view her erotic transference to himself as a repetition of her relationship with her father. Spielrein realized the operation of this complex, revealing to Jung her longing for someone, potentially Jung, who would be a substitute parent for her. Spielrein's erotic transference to Jung demonstrated that she looked for her father's love in Jung (Covington, 2003b). In a letter to her mother, Spielrein wrote in 1908:

> Jung recently finished a paper that created a sensation involving the significance of the father in the destiny of the individual. In it, he shows that the choice of the future love object is determined in the first relations of the child to his parents. Jung is for me father and I am mother for him, or the woman who has acted as the first substitute for the mother [his mother came

> down with hysteria when he was two years old]; he became attached to the [substitute] woman. And now he has fallen in love with me, a hysteric; and I fell in love with a psychopath, and it is necessary to explain why? (as cited in Covington, 2003b, p. 186)

Yet, Spielrein does explain "why," as she acknowledged, "I have never seen my father as normal" (as cited in Covington, 2003b, p. 186). Thus, through transference, Jung became the substitute father—the normal father figure that she so long sought.

Spielrein made the link between her love for Jung and her earlier experience of attachment to her father. Given the tumultuous character of Spielrein's relationship with her father and mother, love for her was not completely free of a destructive component. It is very likely that this destructive component was subsequently linked to the core idea of her paper, "Die Destruktion als Ursache des Werdens." ("Destruction as the Cause of Coming into Being"), a paper she read in the presence of Freud, before the Vienna Psychoanalytic Society in November 1911. Her presentation introduced the concept of a destructive component as part of the sexual instinct (Covington, 2003a). According to Cremerius (2003), Spielrein was the first psychoanalyst to have "presented the thesis that instinctual life is based on two opposing instincts; the life instinct and the death instinct" (p. 70), a viewpoint shared by Van Waning (1992) and Ovcharenko (1999), among others.

Freud originally rejected her thesis, and it was some eighteen years later that, in a reminiscence of his encounter with Spielrein, he tried to understand why: "I remember my own defensive attitude when the idea of an instinct of destruction first emerged in the psycho-analytic literature, and how long it took before I became receptive to it" (Freud, 1929–1930/1986, p. 120). It has been suggested that Freud's inability to accept her thesis of the existence of two instincts may be due to the fact that Freud "understood the concealed message that behind the abstract theory of destruction lay the actual destruction she had experienced" (Cremerius, 2003, p. 69) when her relationship with Jung, as doctor and lover, came to its abrupt and tragic end. Spielrein's "Destruction" paper was published in 1912 in the *Yearbook for Psychoanalytic and Psychopathological Research.*

The "Destruction" paper of 1912 was not Spielrein's first publication. In 1911, her dissertation, "On the Psychological Content of a Case of Schizophrenia (Dementia Praecox)," had also appeared in the *Yearbook* as the leading paper. It had the distinction of being the first psychoanalytically oriented dissertation to be authored by a woman (Richebächer, 2003, p. 242). Freud and Jung were favourably impressed with her published dissertation. Thus, Spielrein received recognition from two individuals whom she greatly admired. As well, she was able to realize her professional ambitions in becoming a medical doctor, a psychiatrist, and an influential psychoanalyst—a professional whose noteworthy ideas were absorbed by both Freud and Jung within the context of their evolving theories and analytic practices.

According to contemporary scholars of the early history of psychoanalysis (Kerr, 1994; Ovcharenko, 1999; Wharton, 2003), Spielrein's concept of a "destructive drive" was her most significant contribution to psychoanalysis (Covington, 2003a, pp. 6–7). As Ovcharenko (1999), in his study of the development of psychoanalysis in Russia, concludes, "[I]deas and conclusions of this original work [the "Destruction" paper] played a vital part in the development of a psychoanalytically-oriented study of the nature and essence of man and gave its author the reputation of being a competent theoretician of psychoanalysis...Sabina Spielrein...was accepted by psychoanalytic circles as one of the best qualified and successful of the first Russian psychoanalysts" (p. 355).

It has been suggested that her erotic transference to Jung, as well as his countertransference to her, led Spielrein to conceptualize a destructive aspect in the drive to love. The idea of a destructive element is, according to Ovcharenko (1999), "bound up with events of...Spielrein's personal life...[T]he original conception of destruction came to her through her own suffering...from grieving over the 'mad passion' of her love for Jung" (p. 359). Thus, according to Spielrein, within the sexual instinct that embodies the drive to love and reproduce, there is a destructive element, suggesting the dualistic nature of the sexual instinct.

Following Spielrein's presentation of her "Destruction" paper to the Vienna Psychoanalytic Society, Freud wrote a letter to Jung expressing his negative opinion of Spielrein's idea of a destructive component within the sexual instinct (Freud & Jung, 1974). Jung concurred (Covington, 2003a). However, in Freud's *Beyond the Pleasure Principle,* published in 1920, he overcame whatever resistances he might have had about Spielrein's theory of a destructive drive by taking, according to Ovcharenko (1999), the "decisive and very responsible step of postulating the existence [of a]...death instinct [an attraction to death, destruction, and aggression]" (p. 362). Moreover, Freud acknowledged that his concept of the death instinct had indeed been built upon Spielrein's original theory of a destructive drive. Freud said "that a considerable portion of these speculations have been anticipated by Sabina Spielrein" in her "instructive and interesting paper" of 1912 (as cited in Ovcharenko, 1999, p. 362). Spielrein "both anticipated and to some extent initiated a major part of Freud's psychoanalytical discussions of man's fundamental instincts" (Ovcharenko, 1999, p. 362). As well, Jung, in his revised edition of *Transformation and Symbols of the Libido* (1952), acknowledged Spielrein as the originator of the death instinct concept.

In her paper, Spielrein noted the "frequency with which sexual wishes are associated with images of death" (Spielrein, 1912/1994, p. 155). The interweaving of love and death as two antagonistic components within the reproductive drive is linked with her notion that nothing new, a new ego or "I," can come into being without the sacrifice or destruction of the old self.

Thus, Spielrein argued that the ego seeks to maintain its individuality and to fight off anything that would enforce unwanted change. However, as Spielrein remarked, "Close to our desire to maintain our present condition, there lies a desire for transformation" (1912/1994, p. 163). And according to Spielrein's analysis of the destructive component within the sexual-reproductive drive, nothing new can come into being without destruction (transformation) of the old order. In Spielrein's own case, the old order was her illness, while the new order, her new "I," came about through her transference-love to Jung. The echo of Freud's observation is understood here: "psychoanalysis is in essence a cure through love" (as cited in Bettelheim, 1984), suggesting that by replacing the old "I" with a new, healthy "I" through the transference-love, the patient is able to let go of the old symptomatic defenses. However, on the basis of Spielrein's analysis, the old "I" resists change and fights off anything that would bring about a transformation of the illness "I" to a healthy "I" (ego).

It is at this point that Jung could offer a solution to the resistance to change that Spielrein alluded to on the part of the old "I." Jung envisioned the treatment of hysteria as one that involves "introducing some new complex that liberates the ego from the domination by the complex of illness" (as cited in Covington, 2003b, p. 183). In keeping with this view of treatment, it would appear that during the course of her therapy, Spielrein was able to replace the unhealthy ego complex with a "new healthy ego complex," thus freeing herself from the "ominous despot," the unhealthy ego, that so dominated her personality. In my view, the curative factor to which Jung referred came into operation by virtue of the growing attachment that Spielrein developed for him. Spielrein's transference neurosis to Jung set the stage for the replacement-transformation process.

To state it in Freud's terms, the artificial transference neurosis replaced the actual neurosis from which Spielrein suffered. Freud held that the transference neurosis had great therapeutic value, arising in part from the personal influence of the therapist.

> This personal influence is our most powerful weapon. It is the new element which we introduce into the situation and by means of which we make it fluid. The intellectual content of our explanations cannot do it...The neurotic sets to work because he has faith in the analyst and believes him because he acquires a special emotional attitude towards the figure of the analyst...[The] use we make of this particularly large "suggestive" influence [is] not for suppressing symptoms—this distinguishes the analytic method from other psychotherapeutic procedures—but as a motive force to induce the patient to overcome his resistances...[T]he emotional relation with the patient...is, to put it plainly, in the nature of falling in love...[This love] grows exacting, calls for affectionate and sensual satisfaction...[I]t has taken the place

> of the neurosis and...our work has had the result of driving out one form of illness with another. (Freud, 1926/1986, pp. 224–226)

For Jung, it was not only important, as Freud argued, to uncover and work through trauma and thus "drive out one form of illness with another," but as well, through the transference, it was important to enable the patient to experience a different object, which can then be internalized, leading to the strengthening of a new ego complex, thereby replacing the unhealthy ego with its healthy counterpart (Covington, 2003b). New identifications and internalizations that arise in the transference pave the way for a new and stronger ego. However, there may be initial resistance to the emerging new and stronger ego.

The resistance of the unhealthy ego complex may be understood in terms of Freud's position on drives. Freud asserted that all drives are essentially conservative and directed toward the maintenance of inner peace—in Fechner's terms, the need for constancy or stability. Thus, the ego (or "I") may resist any attempt that would upset stability, even at the cost of remaining ill. However, Spielrein did not remain in neurotic misery but recovered from her disabling symptoms, reaching a new stasis with a healthy ego complex.

Against the background of her erotic transference to Jung, and in the context of her notion of destruction (that nothing new can come into being without dissolution of the old), Spielrein was able to recover and differentiate a new healthy ego and free herself from the "ominous despot," i.e., her unhealthy ego complex. From the time that Spielrein was admitted to the Burghölzli Clinic in August 1904 to her eventual discharge in June 1905 and her continued therapy with Jung as an outpatient until 1909, it might be said that Spielrein underwent a remarkable transformation; a new ego emerged, born out of the complex of illness that so beset her. Bettelheim (1990) reminds us that the

> most significant event in Sabina's young life was that whatever happened during her treatment by Jung at the Burghölzli, it *cured* her [emphasis added]... Whatever may be one's moral evaluation of Jung's behavior toward Spielrein, his first psychoanalytic patient, one must not disregard its most important consequence: he cured her from the disturbance for which she had been entrusted to his care. (p. 79)

Following Spielrein's treatment and recovery at the Burghölzli Clinic, "Jung suffered from what seems to have been a psychotic breakdown" (Covington, 2003b, p. 187). Yet, as we have seen, Jung continued to exhibit erotic transferences to his female patients, to the point of including his patient, Toni Wolff, in his domestic household (Covington, 2003b). However, eventually Jung's breakdown led him to confront his "polygamous nature" (as cited in Schultz, 1990, p. 126). In a letter dated December 12, 1908, Jung wrote the following to Spielrein:

> It is my misfortune that I cannot live without the joy of love, of tempestuous ever-changing love in my life. The daimon stands as an unholy contradiction to my

> compassion and sensitivity. When love for a woman awakens within me, the first thing I feel is regret, pity for the poor woman who dreams of eternal faithfulness and other impossibilities, and is destined for a painful awakening out of all these dreams...Give me back now something of the love and patience and unselfishness which I was able to give to you at the time of your illness. Now I am ill... (as cited in Wharton, 2003, pp. 37–38)

Jung acknowledged his illness, an insight that likely came about through his encounter with Spielrein and, as well, recognized that his requirement for "tempestuous ever-changing love" was an inherent feature of his polygamous nature. According to Cremerius (2003), Jung wanted "free love from his mistress [Spielrein]...untainted by bourgeois values, but he also wanted to remain in the safe haven and respectability of a bourgeois marriage...He suffered from being entangled in an unhappy marriage, which he neither could nor would dissolve, and from his addictive dependency on love affairs—his 'daimon'" (p. 67). Jung's "daimon" contributed to his eventual estrangement from Freud.

Upon completion of her medical studies, in the fall of 1911, Spielrein travelled to Vienna and, as we know, was elected a member of the Vienna Psychoanalytic Society that October, being "the second woman doctor," as Freud expressed it at that time, to be inducted into the Society (as cited in Richebächer, 2003, p. 243). By the spring of 1912, Spielrein had taken an active part in the Society, given several lectures, and been published in various psychoanalytic journals. It was then that Freud came to value her contributions and referred patients to her (Richebächer, 2003).

As the collegial relationship between Freud and Spielrein blossomed, the collaborative friendship between Freud and Jung began to fray, with temperamental and theoretical differences mounting. By the spring of 1913, Freud wrote to his colleague, Karl Abraham, formerly of the Burghölzli Clinic, regarding Freud's last visit to Jung at the Burghölzli in Zurich, "I have greatly retreated from him, and have no more friendly thoughts for him. His bad theories do not compensate me for his disagreeable character" (as cited in Richebächer, 2003, p. 244). Just one year later, on July 26, 1914, Freud wrote to Abraham, "[S]o we are at last rid of them, the brutal, sanctimonious Jung and his disciples!" (as cited in Richebächer, 2003, p. 244). Spielrein at this time preserved her relationship with both Freud and Jung and even tried to reconcile the two of them (Richebächer, 2003, p. 244).

The fraying of the Freud-Jung relationship and of Freud's hopes that Jung would be his successor prompted a "group of loyalists" (Breger, 2000, p. 208) to rally around Freud. Headed by the militant Ernest Jones and made up of participants of Freud's inner circle, a secret committee was suggested in June 1912; Jung was excluded from membership (Paskauskas, 1988, p. 7). By May 25, 1913, "Freud presents rings to members of Committee—Jones, Ferenczi, Rank, Abraham, and Sachs—in Vienna" (Grosskurth, 1991, p. xviii). Members of the committee shared ideas with one another and monitored any suspected departure from the basic tenets of psychoanalysis as originally laid down by Freud (Breger, 2000). The committee remained active until 1936, controlling membership in the International Psychoanalytic Society and its branches, determining what could be published in psychoanalytic journals and influencing translations of Freud's work into English. Overall, it was the secret committee, at the time of its formation and active service, that would ensure Freud's legacy and carry Freud's vision of psychoanalysis into the future, a legacy that was guarded as well by Freud's daughter Anna until her death in 1982.

Freud's retreat from Jung was in part influenced by Jung's challenges to Freud's libido theory. It was Jung's intention to broaden the dynamic and motivational basis of psychoanalytical theory above and beyond the dimension of sexuality. As well, he chafed at having to submit to Freud's authority and orthodoxy. Their partnership over the course of six years had been a remarkably fruitful one, from the time they met personally in March of 1907 until personal and professional relations came to a halt in 1913. How ironic that, when Freud and Jung first met in Vienna in March 1907, they spoke for thirteen hours, yet they did not speak to each other at all at the Fourth International Psychoanalytic Congress held in Munich in September 1913 (Kerr, 1994).

It was during the time of the dissolution of the Freud-Jung relationship that Spielrein, in correspondence with Freud, tried to bring about reconciliation between the two men. Spielrein, for example, took care in her correspondence with Freud to portray Jung as blameless in their earlier relationship so that Freud would not take such a dim view of the manner in which Jung had treated his young patient. She interpreted Jung's behaviour as the result of the transference/countertransference process and in doing so, attempted to exonerate him of any wrongdoing. In a letter to Freud dated June 10, 1909, she reminded him, "My dearest wish is that I may separate from him in love" (as cited in Carotenuto, 1982, p. 92). She stayed true to her resolve; from 1910 to 1919, she remained in contact with Jung, largely through correspondence. She further wrote to Freud on April 19, 1914, "In spite of all...I like J. and would like to lead him back into *our* [emphasis added] fold" (as cited in Carotenuto, 1982, p. 112).

In 1908, when the Spielrein-Jung affair was at its most intense, Spielrein had imagined conceiving a child with Jung, a son to be named Siegfried. This imagined son was to be a "great Aryan-Semitic hero" (as cited in Covington, 2003a, p. 5), who would unite the two races which Jung and Freud represented for her. Of course, her wish to conceive a son with Jung did not materialize. When Spielrein alluded to this fantasy to Freud, he made his views quite clear, in a letter written January 20, 1913: "My personal relationship with your Germanic hero has definitely been shattered...[for] since I received that first letter from you,[7] my opinion of him has greatly altered" (as cited in Carotenuto, 1982, p. 118).

7. The letter was dated May 30, 1909, and can be found in Carotenuto (1982, p. 91).

Freud's sentiments were clearly expressed to Jung just weeks before the January 20 communication with Spielrein. On January 3, 1913, Freud wrote the following to Jung:

> I propose that we abandon our personal relations entirely. I shall lose nothing by it, for my only emotional tie with you has long been a thin thread—the lingering effect of past disappointments...I therefore say, take your full freedom and spare me... (as cited in Kerr, 1994, p. 437)

Those "past disappointments" most certainly included the full revelations regarding Jung's treatment of Spielrein. On January 6, 1913, Jung wrote a brief and decisive response to Freud, concluding with a quotation from *Hamlet:* "I accede to your wish that we abandon our personal relations, for I never thrust my friendship on anyone. You yourself are the best judge of what this moment means to you. 'The rest is silence'" (as cited in Kerr, 1994, p. 437).

It has been pointed out that Freud's relationships with Breuer and with Jung ended at much the same juncture. Freud's relationship to Breuer ended for good in 1895 with the conclusion of Anna O.'s treatment, and similarly, Freud's and Jung's relationship ended about two years following Jung's conclusion of Spielrein's treatment (Cremerius, 2003). And yet, Spielrein's relationship with both men endured.

Although the relationships between Spielrein and Jung and between Jung and Freud were destructive in the sense that the termination of these relationships shattered the wishes that each harboured for the other, both relationships produced remarkable personal transformation and professional achievement. Through these relationships, Freud, Jung, and Spielrein came to recognize the power of transference-love, which appeared to permeate analytic and personal encounters. This recognition helped to advance the theory and practice of psychoanalytic psychology. Thus, psychoanalysis, as a method of therapy, unleashes the potential of a transference neurosis and in doing so, sets the stage for the intense emotional reactions that arise in both the doctor and patient, emotional reactions that must be worked through so that the benefits for the patient can be realized. One might argue that transference phenomena occurred not only between Spielrein and Jung but between Freud and Jung as well.

Years after Jung's treatment of Spielrein had ended, Freud astutely separated the benefits resulting from the benevolent bonds of love from the hazards of bondage to erotic demands in the transference:

> The relation of transference...has an opportunity for a sort of after-education of the neurotic...However much the analyst may be tempted to become teacher, model and ideal for other people, he should not forget his task in the analytic relationship...In all his attempts at improving and educating the patient the analyst should respect his individuality...[For] as an authority and a substitute for his parents, as a teacher and educator...we raise the mental processes in his ego to a normal level, transform what has been unconscious and repressed into preconscious material

> and thus return it once more to the possession of the ego. (Freud, 1940/1986, p. 181)

Thus, the therapeutic alliance that was established between Jung and Spielrein had the power to transform both the patient and the therapist, and it was Freud who had provided the psychoanalytic method for that transformation.

However, some might argue, as Novick and Novick (2000) have done, that "all knowledge and theory construction [regarding transference] was based on psychoanalytic observation of the patient. Very little was said about the analyst's reciprocal love for the patient" (p. 189). I would disagree with this last contention. As early as the 1890s, Freud had begun to examine the phenomenon of countertransference, as manifested in the powerful emotional responses that Anna O. and Breuer exhibited toward each other during the course of her therapy. Some years later, Breuer told Freud of his experience with Anna O. and also wrote up the case in *Studies on Hysteria*. Freud concluded that Breuer held "the key in his hand" to transference/countertransference, but was unable to use it, or as Freud said, "he dropped it" (as cited in Gay, 1988, p. 67). By the time Jung discussed Spielrein's case with Freud, Freud was well aware of the countertransference dynamic and was able to discern it in Jung's relationship to Spielrein.

In the years after Jung's treatment of Spielrein and the rupture between Jung and Freud, Spielrein made her mark in the fields of psychiatry and psychoanalysis as a theoretician and practitioner. However, despite her contributions to psychoanalysis—contributions acknowledged by both Jung and Freud—she remained largely unknown. As Richebächer (2003) reminds us, "in the...history of psychoanalysis we look in vain for Sabina Spielrein" (p. 246). For example, in Ernest Jones's highly regarded standard text *The Life and Work of Sigmund Freud* (1953), Spielrein does not appear. In Peter Gay's monumental work, *Freud* (1988), Spielrein is only given brief mention with regard to her 1912 paper. Nancy Chodorow (1987), who addressed the contributions women have made to the psychoanalytic movement, "forgets her" (Richebächer, 2003, p. 246). Historians of psychoanalysis, such as Richebächer (2003) and Covington (2003a; 2003b), inform us that the lack of acknowledgement of Spielrein in standard works on history of psychoanalysis is "astonishing...since she was the very first woman to have written a doctoral thesis on a psychoanalytic theme, and furthermore hers is the first thesis to be given prominence of being published in the *Jahrbuch* [*Yearbook*]" (Richebächer, 2003, p. 246).

Further, it has been suggested that the omission of Spielrein in standard works on the history of psychoanalysis (e.g., Jones, 1953; Chodorow, 1987; Gay, 1988) may be due to the association of Spielrein with the "break between Freud and Jung in 1913 which was...traumatic for the psychoanalytic movement" (Richebächer, 2003, p. 247). Lothane (1996) makes a similar suggestion, that "in some quarters the Freud/Jung split is explained by the old recipe of *cherchez la femme,* blaming Spielrein for causing the trouble between the two men...[when] the Freud/Jung split had other causes"

(p. 203) that had nothing to do with Spielrein's relationship with either of these two men. It is more likely that Spielrein's omission has something to do with her personality, for in the patriarchal structures of psychoanalysis, Spielrein, by virtue of her independent spirit, caused offence again and again. According to Richebächer (2003), Ernest Jones, the one-time president of the International Psychoanalytic Association, had a particular dislike for her and so disregarded anything she might have offered the movement. As Richebächer said, Jones, "could not stand her" (p. 247). Thus, Spielrein was relegated to oblivion.

If "the rest is silence" as far as Jung was concerned in his farewell letter to Freud, the same cannot be said of Spielrein. As history has shown, Spielrein was not silent in her relationship with either man; her voice continued to resonate in her correspondence with Jung until 1919 and with Freud until 1923 (Covington, 2003a). At the early age of fifteen years, Spielrein wrote in her diary, "I was looking for a friend to whom I could bare my soul" (as cited in Carotenuto, 1982, p. 25). Perhaps, for a time, she found that friend in Jung and later in her professional relationship with Freud. As Kerr (1994) remarked, "[B]y listening in a new way, psychoanalysis gave...patients a voice they had not known before" (p. 13). It may well be that the manner of listening that psychoanalysis brought to the treatment of neurosis, a manner first discovered by Breuer and Anna O. and later developed by Freud and adopted by Jung for his first psychoanalytic test case, gave Spielrein the permission to finally bare her soul. Through self-disclosure and in the dynamic set in motion through transference/countertransference, Spielrein was able to benefit enormously from what psychoanalytic therapy had to offer. She recovered from a crippling neurosis and this recovery paved the way for her vocation in psychoanalysis and the contributions she was to make to the discipline that transformed her life and work.

Although Spielrein has been overlooked at times, she has not been forgotten. It is hoped that this book makes a contribution to restoring the memory of Spielrein as an important contributor to the early development of psychoanalysis. In the matter of Sabina Spielrein, may the rest no longer be silence.

References

Abraham, H. C. & Freud, E. (Eds.). (1965). *A Psycho-analytic dialogue: The letters of Sigmund Freud and Karl Abraham, 1907–1926*. London: Hogarth and Institute of Psychoanalysis.

Aguayo, J. (2012). Freud, Jung, Sabina Spielrein and the countertransference: David Cronenberg's A Dangerous Method. *The International Journal of Psychoanalysis, 94*(1), 169–178. doi:10.1111/j.1745-8315.2012.00629.x

Allain-Dupré, B. (2004). Sabina Spielrein: A bibliography. *Journal of Analytical Psychology, 49*, 421–433.

Appignanesi, L., & Forrester, J. (2000). *Freud's women*. New York, NY: The Other Press.

Baker, R. R., & Bellis, M. A. (1995). *Human sperm competition: Copulation, masturbation and infidelity*. London, UK: Chapman & Hall.

Bettelheim, B. (1983). Scandal in the family. *The New York Review of Books*, June 30.

Bettelheim, B. (1984). *Freud and man's soul*. New York, NY: Vintage Books.

Bettelheim, B. (1990). *Freud's Vienna and other essays*. New York, NY: Alfred A. Knopf.

Breger, L. (2000). *Freud: Darkness in the midst of vision*. New York, NY: Wiley.

Breger, L. (2009). *A dream of undying fame: How Freud betrayed his mentor and invented psychoanalysis*. New York, NY: Basic Books.

Breuer, J., & Freud, S. (1957). *Studies on hysteria*. (J. Strachey, Trans.). New York, NY: Basic Books. (Original work published 1895)

Buss, D. M. (2012). *Evolutionary psychology: The new science of the mind*. (4th ed.). Boston, MA: Allyn and Bacon.

Carotenuto, A. (1982). *A secret symmetry: Sabina Spielrein between Jung and Freud*. New York, NY: Pantheon.

Casey, S. & Woody, J. M. (1983). Hegel, Heidegger, Lacan: The Dialectic of Desire. In J. H. Smith, & W. Kerrigan (Eds.), *Interpreting Lacan* (pp. 75–112). New Haven, CT: Yale University Press.

Chodorow, N. (1987). Der beitrag der frauen zur psychoanalytischen bewegung und theorie ("Women's contribution to the psychoanalytic movement and to psychoanalytic theory"). *Psyche: Zeitschrift für Psychoanalyse und Ihre Anwendungen 41*(9): 800–831.

Covington, C. (2003a). Introduction. In C. Covington & B. Wharton (Eds.), *Sabina Spielrein: Forgotten pioneer of psychoanalysis* (pp. 1–14). New York, NY: Brunner-Routledge.

Covington, C. (2003b). Comments on the Burghölzli hospital records of Sabina Spielrein. In C. Covington & B. Wharton (Eds.), *Sabina Spielrein: Forgotten pioneer of psychoanalysis* (pp. 177–190). New York, NY: Brunner-Routledge.

Covington, C. (2012). Mutual madness: The erotic transference between Jung and Spielrein. *Couple and Family Psychoanalysis, 2*(2), 233–238.

Covington, C. & Wharton, B. (Eds.). (2003). *Sabina Spielrein: Forgotten pioneer of psychoanalysis*. New York, NY: Brunner-Routledge.

Cremerius, J. (2003). Foreword to Carotenuto's *Tagebuch einer heimlichen Symmetrie*. In C. Covington & B. Wharton (Eds.), *Sabina Spielrein: Forgotten pioneer of psychoanalysis* (pp. 63–80). New York, NY: Brunner-Routledge.

Dawkins, R. (1976). *The selfish gene*. Oxford, UK: Oxford University Press.

Dawkins, R. (1986). *The blind watchmaker*. New York, NY: Norton.

Etkind, A. M. (1997). *The Eros of the impossible: The history of psychoanalysis in Russia*. (N. Rubins, & M. Rubins, Trans.). Boulder, CO: Westview Press.

Falzeder, E. (1998). Family tree matters. *Journal of Analytic Psychology, 43*, 127–154.

Fancher, R. E. (1973). *Psychoanalytic psychology: The development of Freud's thought*. New York, NY: Norton.

Fechner, G. T. (1966). *Elements of psychophysics* (Vol. 1). New York, NY: Holt, Rinehart and Winston. (Original work published 1860)

Freud, S. (1985). *The complete letters of Sigmund Freud to Wilhelm Fliess, 1887-1904* (J. Masson, Ed. & Trans.). London, UK: The Belknap Press.

Freud, S. (1986). *Project for a scientific psychology*. In J. Strachey (Ed. & Trans.), *The standard edition of the complete psychological works of Sigmund Freud* (Vol. 1, pp. 283–397). London, UK: Hogarth Press. (Original work published 1895)

Freud, S. (1986). *The interpretation of dreams*. In J. Strachey (Ed. & Trans.), *The standard edition of the complete psychological works of Sigmund Freud* (Vols. 4–5, pp. 1–627). London, UK: Hogarth Press. (Original work published 1900–1901)

Freud, S. (1986). *Fragment of an analysis of a case of hysteria.* In J. Strachey (Ed. & Trans.), *The standard edition of the complete psychological works of Sigmund Freud* (Vol. 7, pp. 3–122). London, UK: Hogarth Press. (Original work published 1905)

Freud, S. (1986). *The future prospects of psycho-analytic therapy.* In J. Strachey (Ed. & Trans.), *The standard edition of the complete psychological works of Sigmund Freud* (Vol. 11, pp. 141–151). London, UK: Hogarth Press. (Original work published 1910)

Freud, S. (1986). *Instincts and their vicissitudes.* In J. Strachey (Ed. & Trans.), *The standard edition of the complete psychological works of Sigmund Freud* (Vol. 14, pp. 111–140). London, UK: Hogarth Press. (Original work published 1915)

Freud, S. (1986). *Beyond the pleasure principle.* In J. Strachey (Ed. & Trans.), *The standard edition of the complete psychological works of Sigmund Freud* (Vol. 18, pp. 3–64). London, UK: Hogarth Press. (Original work published 1920)

Freud, S. (1986). *The question of lay analysis.* In J. Strachey (Ed. & Trans.), *The standard edition of the complete psychological works of Sigmund Freud* (Vol. 20, pp. 224–226). London, UK: Hogarth Press. (Original work published 1926)

Freud, S. (1986). *Civilization and its discontents.* In J. Strachey (Ed. & Trans.), *The standard edition of the complete psychological works of Sigmund Freud* (Vol. 21, pp. 57–145). London, UK: Hogarth Press. (Original work published 1929–1930)

Freud, S. (1986). *An outline of psychoanalysis.* In J. Strachey (Ed. & Trans.), *The standard edition of the complete psychological works of Sigmund Freud* (Vol. 23, pp. 141–207). London, UK: Hogarth Press. (Original work published 1940)

Freud, S. (1933). *The interpretation of dreams.* (A. A. Brill, Trans.). New York, NY: Macmillan. (Original work published 1900)

Freud, S. & Jones, E. (1993). *The complete correspondence of Sigmund Freud and Ernest Jones, 1908–1939* (R. A Paskauskas, Ed.). Cambridge, MA: Harvard University Press.

Freud, S. & Jung, C. G. (1974). *The Freud/Jung letters: The correspondence between Sigmund Freud and C. G. Jung* (W. McGuire, Ed.). Princeton, NJ: Princeton University Press.

Gay, P. (1988). *Freud: A life for our time.* New York, NY: W. W. Norton.

Graf-Nold, A. (2003). The Zürich School of Psychiatry in theory and practice: Sabina Spielrein's treatment at the Burghölzli Clinic in Zürich. In C. Covington & B. Wharton (Eds.), *Sabina Spielrein: Forgotten pioneer of psychoanalysis* (pp. 143–176). New York, NY: Brunner-Routledge.

Grosskurth, P. (1991). *The secret ring: Freud's inner circle and the politics of psychoanalysis.* Toronto, Canada: Macfarlane Walter & Ross.

Heaton, J. M. (2000). *Wittgenstein and psychoanalysis.* Duxford, UK: Icon.

Heaton. J. M., & Groves, J. (1999). *Introducing Wittgenstein.* London, UK: Icon.

Jones, E. (1953). *The life and work of Sigmund Freud: The formative years and the great discoveries, 1856–1900* (Vol. 1). New York, NY: Basic Books.

Jones, E. (1961). *Sigmund Freud: Life and work.* L. Trilling & S. Marcus (Eds.). New York, NY: Basic Books.

Jung, C. G. (1952). Symbols of transformation. In M. Fordham (Ed.), *Collected works of C. G. Jung* (Vol. 5). Princeton, NJ: Princeton University Press.

Jung, C. G. (1973). Experimental observations on the faculty of memory. In M. Fordham (Ed.), *Collected works of C. G. Jung: Symbols of transformation* (Vol. 2). Princeton, NJ: Princeton University Press. (Original work published 1905)

Kandel, E. (2012). *The art of insight*. New York, NY: Random House.

Kerr, J. (1994). *A most dangerous method: The story of Jung, Freud, and Sabina Spielrein*. New York, NY: Vintage Books.

Launer, J. (2011). *Sex versus survival: The story of Sabina Spielrein: Her life, her ideas, her genius*. www.lulu.com.

Liebert, R. M., & Spiegler, M. D. (1998). *Liebert & Spiegler's personality: Strategies and issues*. Pacific Grove, CA: Brooks/Cole Publishing Co.

Lothane, Z. (1996). In defense of Sabina Spielrein. *International Forum of Psychoanalysis, 5*, 203–217. doi: 10.1080/08037069608412741

Lothane, Z. (2003). Tender love and transference: Unpublished letters of C. G. Jung and Sabina Spielrein (with an addendum/discussion). In C. Covington & B. Wharton (Eds.), *Sabina Spielrein: Forgotten pioneer of psychoanalysis* (pp. 191–226). New York, NY: Brunner-Routledge.

Makari, G. (2008). *Revolution in mind: The creation of psychoanalysis*. New York, NY: Harper.

Marchese, F. J. (1995). The place of eugenics in Arnold Gesell's maturation theory of child development. *Canadian Psychology, 36*(2), 89–114.

Miller, M. A. (1998). *Freud and the Bolsheviks: Psychoanalysis in imperial Russia and the Soviet Union.* New Haven, CT: Yale University Press.

Minder, B. (2003a). A document. Jung to Freud 1905: A report on Sabina Spielrein. In C. Covington & B. Wharton (Eds.), *Sabina Spielrein: Forgotten pioneer of psychoanalysis* (pp. 137–142). New York, NY: Brunner-Routledge.

Minder, B. (2003b). Jung's patient at the Burghölzli. In C. Covington & B. Wharton (Eds.), *Sabina Spielrein: Forgotten pioneer of psychoanalysis* (pp. 111–135). New York, NY: Brunner-Routledge.

Moll, J. (2003). Unedited extracts from a diary: Sabina Spielrein; with a prologue by Jeanne Moll. In C. Covington & B. Wharton (Eds.), *Sabina Spielrein: Forgotten pioneer of psychoanalysis* (pp. 16-31). New York, NY: Brunner-Routledge.

Nasio, J. (1988). *Hysteria from Freud to Lacan: The splendid child of psychoanalysis.* (S. Fairfield, Ed. & Trans.). New York, NY: The Other Press.

Novick, J., & Novick, K. K. (2000). Love in the therapeutic alliance. *Journal of the American Psychoanalytic Association, 48,* 189–218.

Ovcharenko, V. (1999). Love, psychoanalysis and destruction. *Journal of Analytical Psychology, 44,* 355–373.

Paskauskas, R. A. (1988). Freud's break with Jung: The crucial role of Ernest Jones. *Free Associations, 11,* 7–34.

Prochnik, G. (2006). *Putnam Camp: Sigmund Freud, James Jackson Putnam, and the purpose of American psychology.* New York, NY: The Other Press.

Richebächer, S. (2003). "In league with the devil, and yet you fear fire?" Sabina Spielrein and C. G. Jung: A suppressed scandal from the early days of psychoanalysis. In C. Covington & B. Wharton (Eds.), *Sabina Spielrein: Forgotten pioneer of psychoanalysis* (pp. 227–250). New York, NY: Brunner-Routledge.

Schultz, D. (1990). *Intimate friends, dangerous rivals: The turbulent relationship between Freud and Jung*. Los Angeles, CA: J. P. Tarcher.

Spielrein, S. (1911). Über den psychologischen Inhalt eines Falles von Schizophrenia (Dementia Praecox). *Jahrbuch Für Psychoanalytische und Psychopathologische Forschungen (Yearbook for Psychoanalytic and Psycholpathological Research), 3*, 465–503.

Spielrein, S. (1912). Die Destruktion als Ursache des Werdens. *Jahrbuch Für Psychoanalytische und Psychopathologische Forschungen, 4*, 465–503. English trans. 1994. Destruction as the cause of coming into being. *Journal of Analytical Psychology, 39*(2), 155–186. doi:10.1111/j.1465-5922.1994.00155.x

Storr, A. (1989). *Freud: A very short introduction*. New York, NY: Oxford University Press.

Szasz, T. (1963). The concept of transference. *International Journal of Psychoanalysis, 38*, 432–443.

Szasz, T. (1990). *Anti-Freud: Karl Kraus's criticism of psychoanalysis and psychiatry*. Syracuse, NY: Syracuse University Press.

Thomas, J. (Producer), & Cronenberg, D. (Director). (2011). *A dangerous method* [Motion picture]. United Kingdom: Recorded Picture Company.

Thurschwell, P. (2009). *Sigmund Freud* (2nd ed.). New York, NY: Routledge.

Van Waning, A. (1992). The works of pioneering psychoanalyst Sabina Spielrein. *International Review of Psycho-Analysis, 19*, 399–414.

Wharton, B. (2003). The letters of C. G. Jung to Sabina Spielrein. In C. Covington & B. Wharton (Eds.), *Sabina Spielrein: Forgotten pioneer of psychoanalysis* (pp. 33–62). New York, NY: Brunner-Routledge.

Index

NOTE: The annotation *n* indicates a footnote

C

D

E

F

K

L

M

N

O

S

About the Author

FRANK J. MARCHESE, PhD, teaches psychology at York University, Toronto, Canada. He has written two articles on the history of psychology, *Freudian Psychology and Art: An Agreeable Partnership?* and *The Place of Eugenics in Arnold Gesell's Maturation Theory of Child Development*. In the field of developmental psychology, he has written *Absent Eyes and Idle Hands: Where Are the Adults?* and in psychology proper, *Readings in Psychology*. He is also interested in Canadian art history and has penned two biographical sketches, *Arthur Dominique Rozaire: Painting Poetically* (in press), and *Helen McNicoll: The Return of Sunlight*. As well, he is the author of three books of verse: *Passion and Promised Vision*, *Verse in the Key of C*, and *Chiaroscuro: Lyrics Light and Dark*. He resides with his family in Toronto.

CORRESPONDENCE: Faculty of Health, Department of Psychology, York University, 4700 Keele Street, Toronto, Ontario, Canada, M3J 1P3
E-MAIL: frankm@yorku.ca

Made in the USA
Middletown, DE
26 July 2017